Trinity, Incarnation,
and Redemption

Edited with Introduction by

Jasper Hopkins
and
Herbert Richardson

HARPER TORCHBOOKS
Harper & Row, Publishers
New York, Evanston, and London

Anselm of Canterbury

Trinity, Incarnation, and Redemption

Theological Treatises

Contents

Preface   vii

Acknowledgments   ix

Abbreviations   xi

Introduction   xiii

Two Letters Concerning Roscelin   1
  (*Epistolae 129 et 136*)

On the Incarnation of the Word   5
  (*Epistola de Incarnatione Verbi*)

On the Virgin Conception and Original Sin   37
  (*De Conceptu Virginali et de Originali Peccato*)

On the Procession of the Holy Spirit   81
  (*De Processione Spiritus Sancti*)

Letters on the Sacraments   135
  (*Epistolae de Sacramentis*)

On the Harmony of the Foreknowledge, the Predestination,   152
  and the Grace of God with Free Choice
  (*De Concordia Praescientiae et Praedestinationis et
  Gratiae Dei cum Libero Arbitrio*)

Preface

With the publication of this volume the major works of Anselm of Canterbury are now available in English. Some years ago the editors projected and began translations of the previously neglected treatises in the Anselm corpus. *Truth, Freedom, and Evil* was the first volume to appear (Harper & Row, 1967). It contains three of Anselm's early dialogues on philosophical themes. Following this beginning, the editors invited several doctoral students to form a graduate seminar and to share in the translation project. Each of these students, working alone or in pairs, undertook a draft of one of the writings in the present volume. This draft became the basis for further revision, first by the editors and then, as circumstances allowed, in renewed collaboration with the students. For the sake of standardized style and vocabulary throughout these translations, the editors have had to exercise overall authority in determining final readings. But, in general, this volume has been a continuing cooperative affair. We are grateful to the original seminar members for their willingness to persist in this enterprise—even, for most of them, into the early years of their own professorial careers.

Father Maurice Savard, O.M.I., of the Oblate Seminary in Natick, Massachusetts, read through this manuscript. We thank him for his judicious and kind advice. We also acknowledge Thomas Nelson and Sons for permission to translate from F. S. Schmitt's critical edition of the Anselm texts.

Two others deserve special mention: Father Schmitt himself, for his readiness to discuss Anselm, and our friend Maria Grossmann, to whom we dedicate this book.

Jasper Hopkins
Department of Philosophy, University of Minnesota

Herbert Richardson
St. Michael's College, University of Toronto

Acknowledgments

Translated in collaboration with the editors by

GEORGE PECK : *Epistolae 129 et 136*
Epistola de Incarna-
tione Verbi

DOUGLAS JOHNSON and RAY PHYLES : *De Conceptu Virgin-*
ali et de Originali
Peccato

LEE GIBBS and WARREN LEWIS : *De Processione Spiri-*
tus Sancti

LUCIEN RICHARD : *Epistolae de Sacra-*
mentis

G. STANLEY KANE and CHARLES WALDROP : *De Concordia Prae-*
scientiae et Praedes-
tinationis et Gratiae
Dei cum Libero Arbi-
trio.

Abbreviations

DV	*De Veritate*
DL	*De Libertate Arbitrii*
DCD	*De Casu Diaboli*
DIV	*De Incarnatione Verbi*
CDH	*Cur Deus Homo*
DCV	*De Conceptu Virginali*
DP	*De Processione Spiritus Sancti*
DC	*De Concordia*
PL	*Patrologia Latina* (ed. J. P. Migne)
S	F. S. Schmitt, *Sancti Anselmi Opera Omnia* E.g., S–237 :7 (I) indicates p. 237, line 7, vol. I.

Introduction

Anselm of Canterbury (1033–1109) was both philosopher and theologian. During his early monastic years at Bec he came under the tutelage of Lanfranc, who is credited with having revived the study of the *trivium*. At Bec, therefore, Anselm learned the logic of the categorical and the hypothetical syllogism. And together with this formalism he absorbed a lasting concern with grammar—a concern which eventuated in a distinction between proper and improper modes of expression and which led him to take account of the conventions of ordinary language, in the belief that these conventions have a *prima facie* justification. From this point of view his philosophical dialogues on truth, freedom, and evil represent the attempt to avoid "inappropriate words which conceal the truth" and to discover "the genuine truth hidden under the many types of expression" (DCD, 1).

In a loose sense Anselm's first systematic works are more philosophical, his middle and later works more theological. In the *Monologion* and the *Proslogion* he seeks to formulate a decisive philosophical proof of God's existence. *De Grammatico* examines the theory of paronomy; *De Veritate,* the nature of propositions; *De Libertate,* the notion of ability; and *De Casu Diaboli,* the meaning of the word "nothing." Yet even these topics are developed for the sake of theology and as a means to interpreting Scripture rather than treated in and for themselves.[1] Toward the end of his period at Bec and the beginning of his archbishopric at Canterbury, Anselm turned his attention to essentially theological issues, taking up at long last the weighty

---

1. With the exception of *De Grammatico*.

themes of trinity, incarnation, and redemption.[2] *De Incarnatione* (1092–1094) was directed primarily against Roscelin and purports to show that the orthodox notion of triunity in God is rationally consistent, so that it need not give way to either tritheism or modalism. The *Cur Deus Homo* (1094–1098) develops a theory of atonement which breaks with Augustinianism by explaining Christ's death as constituting a returning of honor to God rather than a payment of ransom to Satan. In both *De Incarnatione* and the *Cur Deus Homo* Anselm views the incarnation as the Son of God's assuming a human nature rather than a human person. Jesus is one person in two natures, even as God is three persons in one nature. Anselm does not attempt fully to rationalize these doctrines. The method he utilizes never fails to acknowledge the sphere of mystery into which human intellect cannot penetrate. Yet by appealing to a series of analogies he hopes to elucidate these doctrines enough to show that they are really mysteries and not, after all, self-contradictions or nonsense. In dealing with the issues of trinity, incarnation, and redemption he is self-consciously working out the theology which undergirds the Athanasian Creed. This creed—called variously the Catholic faith and the Quicumque—governs his quest for particular arguments which rationally illumine the basic dogmas of the Christian Church, in so far as this is possible.

In the writings which follow the *Cur Deus Homo* Anselm continues to develop these theological themes. *De Conceptu* (1099–1100) indicates that Jesus was born sinless because He was taken from a virgin by the power of God rather than begotten by the power of the Adamic reproductive nature. Free from original and personal sin alike, Jesus' life could be blameless and His death could make satisfaction for the sins of all other men. *De Processione* (1102) comprises a continuation and extension of the argument of *De Incarnatione*. Directed against the Greeks, it defends the Latin Church's addition of the *filioque*

2. The *Monologion* had already dealt philosophically with the notion of God's triunity.

On the dating of Anselm's works see F. S. Schmitt, ''Zur Chronologie der Werke des hl. Anselm von Canterbury,'' *Revue Bénédictine*, 44 (1932), 322–350.

statement to the Nicene-Constantinople Creed (381). In the face of the accusation that with this change the Western Church distorted the Creed, Anselm contends that not everything which ought to be believed is to be found in the creeds. Moreover, even Scripture itself does not explicitly state that the one God exists in three persons or that the Son exists as God from God. A paramount task of theology, therefore, is to deduce from Scripture, in conjunction with the concept of God as the most perfect conceivable being, those consequences which ought to be believed by the universal church. Since the creeds embody only a portion of these implied doctrines, an addition such as the *filioque* clause does not in itself constitute a corruption or a distortion. In particular, whenever a doctrine can be shown to follow from what Scripture explicitly affirms, with no further reason contradicting it, then its absence from the creeds results from historical rather than from theological considerations. Accordingly, the fact that the Latin Church decided to incorporate into the Creed something which it believed with good reason, represents a process of historical freedom rather than an anomalous theological accretion.

The letters on the sacraments (1106–1107) discuss the symbolism rather than the efficacy of the eucharist. And the subsequent *De Concordia* (1107–1108), which resumes the earlier topic of free will, emphasizes the role of grace as preceding, accompanying, and following the freedom of the faith-act. Moreover, by attempting to reconcile a nonnecessitarian view of choice with the theological doctrines of divine foreknowledge and predestination, this last of Anselm's treatises moves to countermand the view that a person bears no responsibility for his future salvation or condemnation.

Doctrine of Trinity

The doctrine of the Trinity presented in *De Incarnatione* and *De Processione* is indebted primarily to Augustine, through whom Anselm learned to appreciate the distinction between predicates applied to God relationally and predicates applied essentially. Although God is an essential unity, He is also a relation of persons. And what is said about this plurality of persons is not said about God qua God. Thus, for example, God qua God is eternal and underived; but God qua Son is eternally begotten from God the Father. The predicates "God from God" and "God from whom God exists" suffice to distinguish each person in God from the other two. God the Father is "God from whom God exists" since the Son and the Holy Spirit exist from Him. But He is not "God from God," since He exists from no other person. God the Son is "God from God" because He derives from the Father; and He is "God from whom God exists" because the Holy Spirit proceeds from Him as well as from the Father. God the Holy Spirit is "God from God" because He derives from both the Father and the Son; but He is not "God from whom God exists," because no person derives from Him. This system of predicates precludes the possibility of confusing the three persons; for persons cannot be the same unless they have identical predicates. And Anselm has just argued that (in accordance with Scripture) this identity is not the case.

Father	God from whom God exists Not: God from God
Son	God from God God from whom God exists
Holy Spirit	God from God Not: God from whom God exists

Moreover, the Son cannot be the Father, because that which exists from another cannot be the other from which it exists. And, for the same reason, the Holy Spirit can be neither the Father nor the Son. Yet the Holy Spirit is what the Father and the Son are—viz., God. And the Son is what the Holy Spirit and the Father are. Each person of the Trinity, therefore, shares those predicates which belong to God essentially (e.g., eternity, omniscience, omnipotence, omnipresence); for each person is God—who is one nature, essence, or substance. In last analysis, then, the three persons do not differ from one another in being God but in the way each is God with respect to the others.

Anselm seeks to reinforce the credibility of this account by introducing an analogy from earthly things. If he can find amid common discourse an instance of speaking of one thing in accordance with three different predicates, then he assumes that it will be less offensive, or at least less strange, to speak of God in accordance with triunity. He poses this example as follows: the Nile is one water; yet we speak of it as a spring, a river, and a lake. The river and the lake are not the spring; the spring and the lake are not the river; and the spring and the river are not the lake. Yet the spring, the river, and the lake are each what the other is—viz., the Nile. And the one is not more the Nile than the other; but each is equally that which the other two are. Moreover, the lake exists from both the spring and the river—as the Holy Spirit exists from both the Father and the Son. This last point (the *filioque* affirmation) must be not only illustrated but also argued. Anselm's argument moves directly to the point. The Holy Spirit exists from the Father in so far as the Father is God. But in so far as the Father is God He is one (essence) with the Son. Therefore, the Holy Spirit exists from the Father *and* the Son.

In general, Anselm's doctrine of the Trinity does not add anything new to Augustine's position. But it does clearly and systematically develop arguments which concentrate on the point at hand. When we remember the diffusion of topics and the lack of sustained and concentrated argument within Augustine's *De Trinitate,* we can be more appreciative of the fact that Anselm singles out crucial issues and handles them tersely but rigorously. The councils of Soissons and Bari became the focus for the trinitarian controversy as it was renewed in the eleventh century. These councils confirmed rather than revised the credal formulations inherited from an earlier era in the life of the Church. Yet the course of this confirmation engendered the theological refinement of those very considerations which had earlier determined the content of the creeds.

Doctrine of Incarnation

The Son of God is said by Anselm to have assumed manhood, or to have assumed human nature (*assumpsit hominem*). In this way a divine nature and a human nature were hypostatically united in the one person of Jesus. In *De Incarnatione* 11 Anselm presents an alternative view in order to point up the issue at hand.

Why doesn't our saying that there are two natures in Christ commit us to saying also that there are two persons? For before the assumption of manhood (*hominis*) God was a person, and He did not cease being a person after He assumed manhood. Moreover, the assumed man (*homo assumptus*) is a person, because every individual man is known to be a person. This means that the person of God who existed before the incarnation is one, and the person of the assumed man is another. Therefore, just as Christ is God and man, so there seem to be two persons in Him.

Anselm rejects this reasoning by reaffirming that the *hominem* which the Son of God assumed was not another person, i.e., another man, but another nature. "For although in Christ one thing is God and another is man, this does not mean that there is one *person* who is God and another *person* who is man. On the contrary, one and the same person is both God and man." Jesus is thus "the assumed man" and "the Son of the Virgin"—both phrases being used as descriptions whereby He may be referred to uniquely. As soon as Jesus was a person He was one person with the Son of God. Anselm emphatically rejects Nestorianism, according to which Jesus is conceived as having had two persons because He had two natures. In place of the hypostatic union of natures into one person, Nestorianism introduces a doctrine of the moral unity of a human person with the divine person. Accordingly, Nestorius agreed to call Jesus *theotokos* (Son of God) only together with calling Him *anthropotokos* (Son of man). While rejecting this teaching, Anselm at the same time rejected Eutychianism, which denied that the two natures in

Jesus were really distinct. Eutyches argued that where there is only one person there can be only one nature. By contrast, Anselm's entire doctrine of atonement is based upon the presupposition that Jesus is the God-man, fully human and fully divine, without confusion of natures. For only then is there a person who, as man, owes a debt on behalf of his race and who, as God, has the ability to repay this debt.

Doctrine of Redemption

On Anselm's view, then, it is impossible that the human nature which was assumed into a unity of person with the Son of God should have been sinful. For a sinful nature would contaminate the person; and if the person of Jesus were stained by sin, His life and death could not have atoned for mankind. In *De Conceptu*, therefore, Anselm attempts to explain how Jesus could have been taken sinlessly from the sinful mass. To be taken sinlessly is the same as to be born without original sin. Anselm equates original sin with the sin which every descendant of Adam inherits when he is born with an Adamic human nature; and he defines this sin as the absence of uprightness from the rational will.

Adam had both a personal and a natural will. Because of the latter he hungered and thirsted. But through the former he chose to eat of the forbidden tree and thereby to satisfy his natural will wrongly. Adam's sin was therefore a personal sin. And this personal sin corrupted his nature, with the result that it could no longer reproduce itself in uncorrupted form. Therefore, by sinning Adam lost justice (i.e., righteousness) not only for himself but also for all his descendants. These descendants inherit a sinful nature, which in turn renders their persons sinful—even though, in the case of infants, they have not yet sinned personally. By inheriting sin they also inherit guilt. An infant who dies unbaptized, Anselm teaches, is condemned on account of original sin. Yet he is not condemned for Adam's sin. For, although Adam's sin is the *cause* of the infant's sin, still, in being an *effect*, the infant's sin is his own, and not Adam's. Although inherited sin in an infant is not as grave as Adam's personal sin, nonetheless it is punishable by exclusion from the Kingdom of God—since no one with any sin at all is admitted into that kingdom.

Anselm thinks of infants as having been in Adam materially and causally, as what comes from a seed is in the seed. All men may be said to have existed in Adam in the sense that they derive existence ultimately from his seed. Through this seed instrumentally, they inherit a nature which is under the necessity of sinning. Accordingly, although the seed itself is not sinful, nevertheless through the seed is transmitted that human nature which is common to all persons descended from Adam. Since Jesus was begotten by the power of the Holy Spirit and not by Adam's seed, He was not begotten with that injustice which Adam lost for mankind. That is, the Son of God assumed His human nature from Mary, who was herself of Adam's lineage. But this nature could not have been sinful, inasmuch as it was not produced by Adamic seed. "For it is absurd that Adam's sin, debt, and penalty should be passed down through a seed which is produced solely by the will of God—a seed which is not produced or brought forth by any created nature, or by the will of any creature, or by a power given by God to anyone else; for in order to beget a man by means of a new power, God takes from a virgin this seed which is free from sin" (DCV, 13). In the *Cur Deus Homo* Anselm argued that Jesus is *most fittingly* born of a virgin who is herself free of sin; thus through faith in the future death of her Son, Mary became purified. In *De Conceptu* he goes on to assert that even had Mary not been pure, still her sin *could not have* passed over unto an offspring begotten efficiently by the immediate power of God. As God miraculously created Adam both just and unburdened by any disadvantage, so He miraculously made Jesus sinless and unburdened by Adam's corruption.

The sinless birth of Jesus makes possible the redemptive program discussed at length in the *Cur Deus Homo*. If salvation does not come to all men, it is because redemption is not a mechanical process which takes place apart from the human will

or in violence of that will. Provision for the salvation of the race
has been made. But each man must claim this provision through
faith in Christ. Anselm wants to show that the divine predestination of which Scripture speaks does not occur except in
cooperation with a man's own choice. His argument in *De
Concordia* begins with the premise that God predestines in
accordance with His foreknowledge—so that if it can be proved
that God's foreknowledge does not interfere with a man's freedom, then it will follow *a fortiori* that neither does predestination interfere. Anselm's method of proof involves the postulation
of the statement of foreknowledge together with the statement of
freedom. If from these two statements no contradiction can be
elicited, then there can be no objection to subscribing to both at
the same time. Assume, then, that a given human action is to be
freely done. Assume also that God foreknows this action. Now, it
is undeniable that what God foreknows is certain to occur in the
future; otherwise it would be false to say that He *foreknows* it.
It is therefore certain that a human action is to be freely done.
Since this conclusion involves no contradiction, Anselm consistently maintains that God's foreknowledge is a guarantor rather
than a usurper of human freedom. In other words, one who
denies that the will is free must do so on grounds which are
independent of the doctrine of divine foreknowledge and predestination. (And in the earlier *De Libertate* Anselm has stated
his reasons for thinking that these other grounds cannot be
found.)

Conclusion

Anselm's teachings concerning trinity, incarnation, and redemption are no mere rehearsal of his predecessors' views.
Although the Augustinian influence, in particular, makes itself
felt at every turn, Anselm modifies Augustine rather than drawing upon him uncritically. In the world of late eleventh- and
early twelfth-century systematic theology, Anselm stands as the
foremost figure in the Latin medieval church. His mark on his

own generation and on the generation of his successors never
reached the height of eclipsing Augustine. Nevertheless, the unity
and consistency of his theological argument, erected in part upon
a Boethian-Aristotelian base, make him both an original thinker
and a synthetic figure. Where he is wrong he is never foolishly
wrong. If he could not escape the more problematical features of
the intellectual milieu of his time, let it be said to his credit that
he self-consciously worked to perfect that milieu rather than
allowing himself to be quietly carried along by it.

*Trinity, Incarnation,
and Redemption*

Two Letters
Concerning Roscelin

To John the Monk (*Epistola 129*)

To my lord and beloved brother John, your brother Anselm
sends the wish that you may always progress toward better
things.

Because I wanted to discuss at length the problem you mentioned in the letter you were pleased to send me, I have put off
replying until this occasion.[1] You mentioned a certain man [viz.,
Roscelin] who asserts this alternative: that either (*a*) the three
persons in God are three things or else (*b*) the Father and the
Holy Spirit were incarnate together with the Son. Since I received your letter, I have been hindered by many demands on my
time, and I have not been permitted to write the lengthy reply
that I wished. So I am now writing briefly—though if God
deigns to give me an opportunity in the future, I intend to treat
the matter more fully.

There are two ways this man might intend us to understand
his statement that the three persons of God are three things:
either (*a*) as referring to three relations, i.e., as referring to God
in so far as He is the Father, the Son, and the Spirit who proceeds from the Father and the Son; or (*b*) as referring to God in

---

1. This letter and the letter to Bishop Fulco were written between
1090–1092.

so far as He is God. But if he is saying that the three relations are themselves three things, then his assertion is superfluous. For no one denies that in this manner the three persons are three things—provided, however, that it be carefully understood how these relations are called things, what kind of things they are, and whether or not such relations have an effect on the substance in the way that many accidents do. It seems, however, that this is not the way in which he understands these three things, because he adds that the three persons have one will and power. For it is not with respect to their being relations that the three persons have one will and power; rather, it is with respect to their being one God. But if he says that the three persons of God are three things in so far as each person is God, then either he intends to affirm that there are three gods or else he does not understand what he is saying. For the time being, let this suffice to show you what I think about his opinion.

With regard to your request that you might dwell with me before you set out for Rome, be assured that because of my love for Your Honor, I would gladly be willing. But because of the many demands on my time, I don't see that it would be very useful for you. Moreover, it might even be a hindrance to you; for it is clear to me that unless you remain with the bishop until the time of your departure, he will be little or no help to you in determining what you ought to do. And I am not able to do anything that would help you concerning your trip.

Farewell.

To Bishop Fulco of Beauvais (*Epistola 136*)

To my well beloved lord and friend, the venerable Bishop Fulco of Beauvais, brother Anselm, by title abbot of Bec, sends greeting.

Although I am not able to believe the report without reservation, I hear that the cleric Roscelin is saying that either the three persons in God are three things, separate from one another like three angels (in such a way, however, that there is but one will and one power), or else the Father and the Holy Spirit were incarnate [together with the Son]. He asserts further that if custom allowed, we could truly say that there are three gods. Moreover, he also alleges that this was the opinion of Archbishop Lanfranc, of venerable memory,[2] and is now mine.

I have heard that a council[3] is being called in the near future by Rainaldus, the venerable archbishop of Rheims, in order to deal with this matter. Therefore, since I anticipate that Your Reverence will be present there, I would like to indicate to you what reply ought to be made on my behalf if such should be necessary.

As far as Archbishop Lanfranc is concerned—since nothing like this was ever said about him before—his life, known to many religious and wise men, is sufficient to excuse him from the charge that is made. And his absence and death prohibit any new accusation against him. But I wish everyone to be aware of my true position. I hold all those things which we confess in the creeds that begin with the following words:[4] "I believe in God the Father Almighty, Creator of heaven and earth"; "I believe in one God, Father Almighty, Maker of [heaven and earth and of all things visible and invisible]"; and "Whoever wishes to be saved: before all things it is necessary that he hold the Catholic faith." I believe these three bases of the Christian confession with my heart, and I confess them with my mouth; hence I am certain that any man or angel who wants to deny any part of them is anathema—and this applies expressly to anyone who affirms as the truth that blasphemy which I have heard is uttered by Roscelin. And to confirm this, I add: let him remain anathema as long as he persists in this obstinacy—for he is not a Christian at all.

Now if such a person was baptized and brought up a Christian,

2. Lanfranc died in May, 1089.
3. The council of Soissons, which condemned Roscelin in 1092.
4. Viz., the Apostles' Creed, the Nicene-Constantinople Creed, and the Quicumque.

he ought not even be given a hearing. And not even a defense of his error should be demanded from him, nor should we offer any argument to him in behalf of the truth we affirm. But as soon as his falsehood has been recognized beyond doubt, either let him anathematize the poison which he produces and vomits forth or else let him be anathematized by all Catholics—unless he recants. For it is utterly foolish and pointless to bring back into the uncertainty of puzzling questions what is firmly established upon solid rock—to do so at the behest of every man who lacks understanding. Our faith ought to be defended by reason against the impious, but not against those who admit that they delight in the honor of being called Christian. For while to the former it should be shown rationally that they irrationally despise us, from the latter it is right to require that they hold firmly to the pledge taken at their baptism. A Christian should advance through faith to understanding, not come to faith through understanding, or withdraw from faith if he cannot understand. Rather, when he is able to attain to understanding, he is delighted; but when he cannot, he reveres what he is not able to grasp.[5]

I request that this letter of mine be taken by Your Holiness to the council I mentioned; or, if by chance you should not be going, that it be sent through one of your clerics. If an explanation of Roscelin's appeal to my name is required, let my letter be read in the hearing of the whole gathering. But if no such explanation is demanded, there will be no need for this letter to be produced.

Farewell.

---

5. The distinction here between offering the non-Christian an apologetic and offering the Christian an exhortation is important for interpreting Anselm's doctrine of *fides quaerens intellectum*.

On the Incarnation
of the Word
(*Epistola de Incarnatione Verbi*)

To the supreme Pontiff Urban, Lord and Father of the universal church in its earthly sojourn, Brother Anselm, sinner in life, monk in habit, called to be bishop of the chief city Canterbury (by either the command or the permission of God), offers due subjection, with humble service and devout prayers.

I

Divine providence has chosen Your Holiness, and has appointed you custodian of the Christian faith and life, and ruler of the Church. Therefore, if anything arises in the Church which is contrary to the Catholic faith, there is no one besides yourself to whom such a matter is more rightly to be referred for authoritative correction. And, further, if anyone prepares a response to error, you are the one to whom it is most safely to be referred for prudent scrutiny. Nothing could be more appropriate, therefore, than that I should send the present letter to Your Wisdom, and this I do most willingly. For if anything in it needs to be corrected, you will set it right by your judgment; and where it holds to the rule of truth, you will confirm it by your authority.

When I was still abbot at the monastery in Bec, the following assertion was advanced by a certain cleric in France: "If the three persons in God are only one thing (*res*), and not three things, each separate in itself, like three angels or three souls—being one in such a way, however, that the three are wholly the same in will and power—then the Father and the Holy Spirit were incarnate with the Son."[1] When this error was brought to my attention, I began a letter against it. However, I neglected to complete it, even though a part of it had been written. For since he against whom it was being written had abjured his error in the council[2] called by the venerable Archbishop Rainaldus of Rheims, and since there did not seem to be anyone who was unaware that this man had been mistaken, I thought there was no need for it. (That part of the letter which I had written was, however, transcribed by certain brothers, without my knowledge, and passed on to others to read. I mention this so that if this part should come into anyone's hand, then although there is nothing false in it, it should nevertheless be regarded as incomplete and unpolished. For what I began there needs to be more carefully undertaken and completed.)[3]

Now, after I was seized and bound to the episcopate of Canterbury by some unfathomable disposition of God, I heard that the author of the above-mentioned novelty was persisting in his opinion and was saying that he had only abjured what he had said before because he was afraid he would be killed by the people. For this reason, certain brothers petitioned me, urging that I should solve the problem (*questionem*) in which he was so entangled that he believed he could extricate himself only by affirming either the incarnation of God the Father and God the

1. In this treatise Anselm nowhere refers to Roscelin by name. It is clear, however, whom he has in mind. (Cf. the letters to Bishop Fulco (No. 136) and John the Monk (No. 129)). Anselm does not seem actually to have had firsthand contact with Roscelin's views, but to be relying upon verbal and written reports. In section XI of the present treatise he explicitly acknowledges the limitation of his acquaintance.

2. *Supra*, p. 3, n. 3.

3. See F. S. Schmitt, "Cinq recensions de l'*Epistola de Incarnatione Verbi* de S. Anselme de Cantorbéry," *Revue Bénédictine*, 51 (1939), 275–287.

Holy Spirit, or else a plurality of gods. And I, in turn, petition that no one think me so bold as to believe that the strength of the Christian faith needs the assistance of my defense. Indeed, if a wretched, insignificant man like me were to try to write something to strengthen the foundation of the Christian faith, as if it stood in need of my defense, when there are so many wise and holy men everywhere, then I could justly be called presumptuous and be made to look a laughing stock. For if other men saw me loaded with stakes and ropes and the customary things used to tie down and stabilize what is liable to collapse, and if they saw me working around Mount Olympus in order to strengthen it and prevent it from tottering and being destroyed by some kind of shock, it would be amazing if they could restrain themselves from laughter and derision. How much more would this happen if I tried, with my arguments, as though I were going to stabilize something that was tottering, to prop up that stone which was "cut out from a mountain by no human hand and which struck and smashed the statue" which Nebuchadnezzar saw in a dream, that stone which has now become "a great mountain and has filled the whole earth" (Dan. 2:34 f.)? Wouldn't those holy and wise men, who rejoice because they have their lives founded upon this mountain's eternal stability, be entitled to be indignant with me and to consider my effort to be the result not of serious learning but of frivolous boasting? Therefore, if in this letter I deal with anything that has to do with the stability of our faith, it is not for the sake of confirming that stability but for the sake of satisfying the requests of my brethren who asked for the discussion.

But if the one who expressed the above-mentioned opinion has already been corrected by God and returned to the truth, then he should in no way consider that I am speaking against him in this letter, since he is no longer what he was. For if he was "once darkness, but is now light in the Lord" (Eph. 5:8), we ought not to accuse the darkness which no longer exists but to approve the light which now shines. And yet, whether he has returned to the light or not, I perceive that there are many who struggle with the same problem. And even though their faith surmounts the reasoning which to them seems inconsistent with that faith, I do not think it superfluous to resolve this inconsistency.

But before I examine this question, I will undertake a preliminary discussion in order to curb the presumption of those who, with blasphemous boldness and on the ground that they cannot understand it, dare to argue against something that is confessed by the Christian faith. For instead of acknowledging with humble wisdom that it is possible for many things to exist which they are not able to comprehend, such men judge with foolish pride that nothing can exist which they cannot understand. But clearly no Christian ought to debate whether something which the Catholic Church believes with its heart and confesses with its mouth is false. On the contrary, by clinging constantly and unhesitatingly to this same faith, by loving it and living humbly according to it, the Christian ought to search for the reason which shows why this faith is true. If he is able to understand, then let him give thanks to God. But if he cannot, then instead of tossing it about with his horns, let him bow his head in veneration before it. For when self-confident human wisdom pits its horns against this stone, it can uproot them more quickly than it can roll the stone. When some men are just beginning to learn, they have a habit of glorying in the power of a knowledge which has confidence in itself, and they presume to rise up to the highest questions of the faith before they possess, through firmness of faith, the requisite spiritual wings. And they are unaware that someone might consider that he knows something, without yet having learned the proper manner in which he ought to know it. The result is that as long as, through prior understanding, they try to attain those things which first require the ladder of faith, they invert the order prescribed in the text, "Unless you believe, you will not understand" (Is. 7:9),[4] and are forced to descend into all sorts of errors because their understanding is defective. For it is clear that they have no

---

4. "*Nisi credideritis, non intelligetis.*" The Vulgate reads: "*si non credideritis, non permanebitis.*" Anselm, like Augustine, is following the Old Latin translation of the Septuagint. Cf. Augustine, *De Trinitate*, Bk. 15 (PL, 42:1058).

foundation of faith who, because they cannot understand what they believe, argue against the truth of the same faith as was confirmed by the holy Fathers. It is just as if bats and owls, who see the sky only at night, were to dispute about the midday rays of the sun with eagles, who with unblinded vision gaze directly at the sun.

Before we apply our judgments to the investigation of the deep things of the faith, therefore, several conditions must be fulfilled. The heart must be cleansed by faith, in accordance with the way in which God is spoken of as "cleansing their hearts by faith" (Acts 15:9). And the eyes must be enlightened through the keeping of the precepts of the Lord, because "the precept of the Lord is light, enlightening the eyes" (Ps. 19:8). And we ought to become as little children through humble obedience to the testimonies of God, in order that we might learn that wisdom which the testimony of the Lord gives, testimony which is faithful, "making wise the simple" (Ps. 19:7). It is from this standpoint that the Lord says: "I thank thee, Father, Lord of heaven and earth, that You have hidden these things from the wise and prudent and have revealed them to little ones" (Matt. 11:25). Then, finally, we must live according to the Spirit, putting aside the things of the flesh. For whoever lives according to the flesh is carnal or natural (*animalis*), and of such it is said that "the natural man does not perceive the things which are of the Spirit of God" (I Cor. 2:14). But he who by the Spirit "puts to death the deeds of the body" (Rom. 8:13) is made spiritual, and it is written of him that "the spiritual man judges all things, but is himself judged by no one" (I Cor. 2:15). For it is true that the more richly we are fed on those things in sacred Scripture which nourish us through obedience, the more deeply we are carried on to those things which satisfy through understanding. It is vain for someone to try to reply: "I have understood more than all my teachers" (Ps. 119:99), when he does not dare to add: "for Thy testimonies are my meditation" (Ps. 119:99). And he speaks untruthfully if he says, "I understand more than the ancients," when he is unaware that this text goes on: "for I have sought Thy commandments" (Ps. 119:100).

Certainly this is exactly what I am saying: he who does not believe will not understand. For he who does not believe will not experience, and he who has not had experience will not know. For the knowledge of one who experiences is superior to the knowledge of one who hears, to the same degree that experience of a thing is superior to hearing about it.

And not only is the mind prevented from rising to the understanding of higher things when it lacks faith and obedience to the commandments of God, but by the neglect of good conscience even the understanding which has already been given to a man is sometimes removed and faith itself overturned. For the Apostle says of some: "When they knew God, they did not honor Him as God or give thanks to Him; but they became futile in their thinking, and their foolish hearts were darkened" (Rom. 1:21). And when the Apostle instructed Timothy "to fight the good fight," he said "to have faith and a good conscience, for, rejecting conscience, some men have made shipwreck of their faith" (I Tim. 1:18 f.). Therefore, let no one plunge rashly into complex questions concerning divine things. Let him first, in firmness of faith, strive for earnestness of life and of wisdom, lest, running through a misleading mass of sophistries with frivolous lack of care, he be trapped by some persistent falsehood.

All men are to be warned that they should approach questions concerning the Sacred Page with the utmost caution. Certainly those dialecticians of our time (or, rather, the "heretics of dialectic") who think that universal substances are mere words (*flatum vocis*), and who are not able to understand color as something different from a material object, or human wisdom as something different from the soul, ought to be blown right out of the discussion of spiritual questions. Indeed, in the souls of these men, reason—which ought to be the ruler and judge of all that is in man—is so covered over by corporeal images that it cannot extricate itself from them and cannot distinguish from among them those things which ought to be considered purely and in isolation. For how can someone who does not yet understand how several men are one man in species comprehend how in that highest and most mysterious Nature several persons—each one of whom is perfect God—are one God? And how can someone whose mind is so dark that it cannot distinguish between his own horse and its color distinguish between the one God and His several relations? Finally, whoever can understand the word "man" (*hominem*) to designate only an individual must interpret this word to mean only a human person—for every individual man is a person. But how then will he understand that the manhood (*hominem*) assumed by the Word was not a person?[5] For it was another nature, not another person, which the Word assumed.

I have said these things in order that no one should presume to discuss the highest questions of faith before he is ready; or, if he should presume to do so, in order that no difficulty or impossibility of understanding should be able to shake him from the truth to which he has held by faith. But now we must come to the matter on account of which we began this letter.

II

This man who is said to maintain that the three persons of the Trinity are like three angels or three souls also says, so I hear: "The pagans defend their law; the Jews defend theirs. Therefore, we Christians ought also to defend our faith." Let us hear how this Christian defends his faith: "If," says he, "the three persons are only one thing, and not three things, each separate in itself, like three angels or three souls—being one, in such a way, however, that the three are wholly the same in will and power—then the Father and the Holy Spirit were incarnate with the Son." Look closely at what this man says—at how this Christian defends his faith! Obviously he either wants to confess that there are three gods or he does not understand what he is saying. But if he confesses that there are three gods, he is not a Chris-

---

5. The word *homo* is herein translated contextually as "man," "manhood," "the man," "a man." God the Son assumed manhood; but the assumed man is Jesus. For a discussion of the problems surrounding the lack of a definite article in Latin syntax, see Anselm of Canterbury, *Truth, Freedom, and Evil*, ed. and trans. J. Hopkins and H. Richardson (New York: Harper & Row, 1967), pp. 76–77.

tian. And if he affirms what he does not understand, he ought not to be given credence.

We should not reply to this man by the authority of Scripture, because he either does not believe Scripture or else he interprets it in a perverse sense. For what does sacred Scripture say more clearly than that there is only one God (*deus unus et solus est*)? His error therefore must be demonstrated by the same reason by which he endeavors to defend himself. In order to do this more easily and briefly, I shall discuss only the Father and Son, because these two persons are clearly signified to be distinct from each other by their own proper names. (For the name "Holy Spirit" is not alien to the Father and the Son, since each of them is both "spirit" and "holy.") However, what we discover concerning the unity of substance or the plurality of persons in the Father and the Son, we shall also know without doubt to be the case in all three.

So, then, suppose my opponent begins by saying: "If the two persons, Father and Son, are not two things (*duas res*) . . . ." Let us ask first what he means by this expression "two things." For we believe that each of the persons is that which is common to both and that which is proper to Himself. The person of the Father is both God (which is common to Him with the Son) and Father (which is proper to Him). Similarly the person of the Son is God (which is common to Him with the Father) and Son (which is said of this person alone). In these two persons, therefore, one thing is common, viz., God, and two things are proper, viz., Father and Son. Now, whatever properties are common to them—such as omnipotence and eternity—are to be understood solely in this common aspect; while such properties as are peculiar to each—such as Begetter or Begetting (for the Father), Word or Begotten (for the Son)—are signified by the two names "Father" and "Son." When my opponent says, therefore, that these two persons are two things, I ask what, in this instance, he is calling two things? Is he talking about what is common to them or about those characteristics which are individually proper to each of them singly? Now, if he says that "two things" here means the two sets of properties, viz., the Father and the Son, so that what is common is only one thing and not several, then he is speaking superfluously—because no Christian confesses that, with respect to these two sets of properties, the Father and the Son are one thing, but rather that they are two. (For we customarily use the word "thing" (*res*) to mean whatever we say is something in some way or other; and whoever calls God Father or Son says of Him that He is something.) Everyone knows that, in God, the Father is not the Son and the Son is not the Father. There is no parallel with those cases in which in one man a father might be a son and a son a father (i.e., where the same man happens to be both a father and a son). With respect to God the terms "Father" and "Son" express a relationship of opposition [viz., a relationship between two persons], but when applied to a single man the terms do not express a relationship between two persons. For, although a man is called father with respect to someone else who is his son, he is called son with respect to a third person who is his father.

Therefore, nothing prevents our saying that the two persons, Father and Son, are two things—provided it is understood what kind of things they are. For the Father and the Son are two things with respect to their relations, not their substance. However, my opponent clearly shows, by what he goes on to add, that this relation is not the way he understands the two persons to be two things. For, having said, "If the three persons are only one thing and not three," he then specifies: "each separate in itself" (*per se separatim*). Indeed, he seems to be setting forth a kind of distinction which would preclude the possibility that the Father and the Son could be together (*simul*) in the same man. Only through such distinction does he think he can free the Father from sharing in the incarnation with the Son. For if he believes that there is only one God, who is Father and Son, he does not see that the Father and the Son can be distinguished (so as not to be together in the same man) according to that distinction by which to be the Father is one thing and to be the Son is another—since paternity and filiation are distinct from each other. Therefore, either (1) he is speaking of another distinction of the persons of the Father and the Son than that by which the

Father and the Son are distinct from each other according to what is proper to each or (2) he is speaking of this same distinction. If the former, then he does not understand by that distinction that the incarnation is alien to the Father; indeed, he thinks that if the Father and the Son are together, it follows that the Father shares in the incarnation with the Son. If the latter, then as I have already said, he is laboring in vain—for this is how the Christian faith understands the Father and the Son to be two things.

Further, by adding "like three angels or three souls," he shows plainly that he is not talking about that distinction which is in these persons according to their properties. Certainly expressions like "two angels" and "two souls" are not used with reference to anything that is numerically one and the same. Nor is anything numerically one predicated of two angels or two souls. But we do call God, who is numerically one, Father and Son; and we do say that the Father and the Son are numerically one God. For we believe and say that God is Father and that God is Son—and, conversely, that the Father is God and that the Son is God. And yet we neither believe nor say that there are several gods, but rather that God is one in number just as in nature, even though the Father and the Son are not one, but two. Now, we use the names "angel" and "soul" substantially, not relationally. It is true, of course, that the name "angel" is taken from a function, since "angel" means "messenger." But it is still regarded as belonging to the category of substance, just like "soul." Therefore, he is talking about the same kind of plurality and separation as several angels or souls have, viz., a substantial plurality. Furthermore, he seems to make this clear when he adds: "in such a way, however, that the three are wholly the same in will and power." For he understands will and power in these several divine things in the same way as in several angels or souls. And this is intelligible only if these several divine things are held to exist in plurality according to that which they are called in common, rather than according to the properties of the persons. For the Father and the Son have no will or power except according to the substance of deity, which is common to both of them. They do not possess will or power at all according to their properties, i.e., according to paternity or sonship. Wherefore, if he means that the three persons are three things according to their own properties, the remark would plainly be superfluous. And when it is taken with "like three angels or souls," it is also inconsistent.

III

But if my opponent is saying that these same persons are two things according to that which is common to both of them, i.e., according to that whereby each singly and whereby all together are one perfect God, then first of all I pose the question of whether he is a Christian. He will reply, I suppose, that he is. In that case he believes that there is one God and that He is three persons—Father, Son, and Holy Spirit. He also believes that only the person of the Son was incarnate, although with the cooperation of the other two. But whoever holds this faith maintains that anyone contradicting it is not a Christian. So then, if he does believe such doctrines, he will deny that anyone arguing against them is a Christian. Let us now go on to consider, however, whether he himself is trying to undermine this faith. (In what follows I shall continue to speak of two persons, on the understanding that what is said will in fact apply to all three.) Now when he says, "If the two persons are one thing and not two (like two angels or two souls), it follows that the Father as well as the Son was incarnate," I think that he is reasoning with himself in the following way:

If God is numerically one and the same thing, and this very same thing is both Father and Son, then when the Son became incarnate, how is it that the Father also was not incarnate? For where two different things are involved, there is no reason why something should not be affirmed of one thing while at the same time it is denied of the other. But if we are speaking of one and the same thing, the affirmation of something and the denial of it cannot both be true at the same time. For example, it is not true that the same Peter both is and is not an apostle. And even if under one name he is affirmed to be an apostle, while under another name this is denied—as, for example, "Peter is an apostle," and, "Simon is not an apostle"—these propositions are not both true. One of them is false. But "Peter is an apostle" and "Stephen is not an apostle" can both be true, because Peter and Stephen are different people. If therefore the Father is numerically one and the same thing as the Son, we cannot truly affirm something of the Son and deny it of the Father, or affirm it of the Father and deny it of the Son. Therefore, whatever the Father is, the Son is also; and what is said of the Son ought not to be denied of the Father. But the Son was incarnate. Therefore, the Father also was incarnate.

Now if this reasoning is valid, then the heresy of Sabellius is true. For if what is said of one person is said also of the other, because the two persons are one thing, then the terms "Son," "Word," and "Begotten," which are applied to the Son, would also apply to the Father. And just as the Father is "Father," "Begetter," and "Unbegotten," so these terms should be used of the Son also. But if this is the case, the Father is not other than the Son, nor the Son other than the Father. And so they are not two persons but one. For they are said to be two persons (if it is granted that God is Father and Son) because the Father and the Son are believed to be distinct from each other. A father is always the father of someone, and a son is always someone's son. No father is ever his own father, nor is a son ever his own son. There is always one who is the father and another of whom he is the father; and similarly with a son. Therefore, if there is not in God one who is the Father and another whose father he is, or one who is the Son and another whose son he is, then God is falsely called Father or Son. For if in God there is not someone other than the Father, of whom the Father is father, then there cannot be a Father; and the same applies to the Son. Thus, there would be no reason for speaking of these two persons in God, since they are in fact thus spoken of as two because God is Father and God is Son, and the Father is always one and the Son always another.

Do you see, therefore, how our faith is destroyed by the opinion of someone who thinks that unless the several persons in

God are several things rather than one, then the Father was incarnate with the Son? For if his inference really follows, then not only what I have said about the Father and the Son will have to be said commonly about all three persons, but there will result such a confusion about all three persons that whatever is said properly of each will also have to be said of all in common. There will therefore be no reason why the Father and the Son and the Holy Spirit, who proceeds from the Father and the Son, should be different from one another (as I have shown by considering the case of the Father and the Son). Therefore, there will not be any relation in God, since a relation exists in no way in God except according to that whereby the persons are distinct from one another. And there will therefore be no plurality of persons. Thus, if it is posited that the three persons are one thing, then either what he says about the incarnation does not follow from this assertion or else all the things that I have just been saying are together entailed by it. For the inference has the same validity in all these cases. So why does he take up the incarnation as if it alone posed a problem? Why does he not rather say: "If the three persons are one thing, then there are not three persons"? For this question can be raised before the incarnation just as much as after it.

IV

However, if he is determined to assert that according to that by which each of the persons is God they are not one thing, but three things, each by itself, like three angels, then it is quite clear that he is setting up three gods. Of course, it may be that he himself does not actually use the words "like three angels or three souls." Perhaps the one who passed the question on to me introduced this example himself, while the man whose views we are discussing affirms only that the three persons are three things without the addition of any illustration. But why, then, is he misled or does he mislead others by the use of the name "thing" (res) when it signifies what the name "God" signifies? Clearly

there are only two alternatives. Either he will deny that God is
that thing in which there are three persons (or rather, as we
confess, that thing which *is* three persons) ; or, if he does not deny
this, his assertion that the three persons are not one thing but
three things must amount also to the statement that these same
persons are not one God but three gods. And let Christians
judge how impious these statements are.

But to this he will respond : ''The fact that I say 'three things'
does not compel me to admit three gods, because these three
things are together one God.'' And I reply that, in that case,
each single one of these things, i.e., each individual person,
would not be God, but God would consist of a combination of the
three things. The Father, therefore, would not be God, nor would
the Son, nor would the Holy Spirit, because God would not be
referred to when one or two of these names are used, but only
when all three are mentioned at the same time. And this is as
impious as the preceding opinions. For if this view were correct,
God's nature would not be simple but composite. Now, if my
opponent's intellect is not complicated and confused by a multiplicity of images, he will understand that, in so far as simplicity
and composition are the points at issue, the simple is superior to
the composite. For, while everything composite must be able to be
divided either in fact or in thought, the same is not true of what
is simple. For no intellect can dissolve into parts anything whose
parts are incapable of being apprehended by thought. It follows,
then, that if God is a composite being made up of three things,
there is either no nature at all which is simple or else there is
some other nature which in some respect is more excellent than
the nature of God. But it is easy to see how false both these
alternatives are. Of course, my opponent may be one of those
modern dialecticians who believe that nothing exists that they
cannot imagine, and so might consider that there is nothing in
which there are no parts. But still, he will not deny that if there
existed something which could be divided neither in fact nor in
thought, it would be greater than something which could be
divided even if only in thought. And from this it follows that,
since everything composite is capable of being divided at least in

thought, then when he says that God is a composite being, he is saying that he is able to conceive something greater than God. His intellect therefore passes beyond God. But that is impossible.

V

But now let us look at what he adds as if to ward off the inconsistency which seems to arise if the three persons are three things: "in such a way, however, that the will and power of these three things is one." Here we must ask: Are these three things divine natures (a) according to what distinguishes them from one another, or (b) according to the will and power which they have in common, or (c) not only because of what they have singly, nor only because of what is common to them, but because of both together? Clearly, as far as (a) is concerned, if they possess deity as a result of that which they are separately, then they will be three gods, and can be discerned as gods without reference to will and power. For individual properties are always understood quite apart from those which are common, and vice versa. But no one is able to understand the divine nature apart from reference to will and power. With regard to (b), if singly and in combination of two or three these three things are God because of one common will and power, then what are these three discordant things doing in the Godhead? For it seems that apart from the agency of some other factor they are not able to harmonize into the unity of deity and do not have the power to bring about the perfection of God, or even to make a contribution to there being a God. For if the one will and power is sufficient for God's perfection, what are these three things which God needs, and why does He need them? For we believe that God needs nothing. There is no point therefore in thinking that these three things are in God. As far as (c) is concerned, if God is constituted not by these three things alone, nor by will and power alone, but by them all together, I repeat that in this case God is composite—God is made up of elements which are not in themselves (*per se*) God or gods. And if he says further that these three things are called God because of power and will in the same way as a man is called a king because he exercises the power of kingship, then "God" is not the name of a substance. Rather, on this basis, these three things (whatever they are) are called three gods accidentally (*accidentaliter*), just as three men with the same power of kingship are called three kings; for three men cannot be one king. I need not say how abominable this view is.

I would have to fill a large book if I wished to write out the absurdities and impieties which follow from the conclusion that because these three persons are one thing according to that which we ascribe in common to the three of them, the incarnation of one person of the Godhead requires the incarnation of the other two as well. And the same could be said of the argument that because only the Son was incarnate, these three persons are three separate things, in the way in which my opponent maintains. It is clear, therefore, that he ought not to be so eager to argue about profound matters—especially when they are such that one cannot err without danger.

VI

But perhaps my opponent will say to me:

My conclusion seems as necessary to me as your further deductions from my conclusion seem to you. Therefore, show that my conclusion does not follow and I will concede to you that no inconsistency arises if the Son alone is incarnate, or if the three persons are one thing. If you fail to do this, you will not solve the problem but only compound it, since you yourself will join me in proving that innumerable inconsistencies result if these assertions are made. Our only escape from these inconsistencies will then be to conclude that if only the Son is incarnate, the three persons are not one thing, or if they are one thing, they were all incarnate in the same way.

I must therefore go on to show where my opponent is being deceived, and how from the incarnation of the Son alone it does not follow that the three persons are three separate things, and to

show that the three persons were not incarnate if the three of
them are only one thing. Now it is certain that the holy Fathers,
especially the most blessed Augustine, following the apostles and
evangelists, have argued with irrefutable reasoning that God is
three persons and is yet only one individual, simple nature. And
even I have written two small works, the *Monologion* and the
Proslogion, which are intended particularly to show that it is possible to prove by necessary reasons, apart from Scriptural authority, those things which we hold by faith concerning the divine
nature and the persons, apart from the incarnation. If anyone is
willing to read these writings, I think he will find in them arguments regarding the matter before us which he will not be able to
disprove and will not want to treat with contempt. My intention
was not to teach what our doctors were ignorant of or to correct
what they did not put well. I have tried, rather, to give expression to things about which, perchance, they were silent, but
which yet are not out of harmony with their teachings but
coherent with them. I have attempted to answer, on behalf of our
faith, those who, while unwilling themselves to believe what they
do not understand, deride others who do believe. And I had
another purpose—to assist the conscientious striving of those
who seek humbly to understand what they already firmly believe.
If in these writings I have said things which I have not read
elsewhere, or which at least I do not remember having read, I do
not think I should be reproached in any way on this account.
However, I do not want to inflict upon the readers of this letter
the task of searching out some other writing in order to know by
clear reason as well as by faith that the three persons are not
three gods but only one, or that the incarnation of God according
to one of the persons does not necessitate that the same God be
incarnate according to the other two. I shall therefore append the
following argument, which I believe is sufficient to refute the
view of this self-styled defender of our faith.

He clearly asserts that either the Father and the Holy Spirit
were incarnate with the Son or else these three persons are three
separate things. Doubtless he understands this "separation" in
such a way that neither the Father nor the Holy Spirit is in the

Son. For if the other two persons are in the Son and the Son is in a man, then they also are in that man. And if the three persons are together in the same man, and if they are one thing, then it is quite impossible for the person of the Son to be *incarnate* in this man without the other two persons being *incarnate* as well. (Nevertheless, my opponent does not deny either that there are three persons or that the Son was incarnate.) Now it has been shown above that if the three persons are three separate things, then either there are three gods or other absurd consequences follow, of which I have already spoken. I will therefore now show briefly, with the help of the one and only God, first of all, that even if there were three gods, this would not keep the Father and the Holy Spirit from being incarnate, although my opponent maintains that apart from positing a multiplicity of gods the other two persons cannot be kept out of the incarnation. After that I will show that there are not many gods but only one. Finally, I will make it clear that although the one God is three persons, the incarnation of any of these persons does not necessitate the incarnation of the others also, but that, on the contrary, this is impossible.

VII

Now it is certain that the divine Nature so exists always and everywhere that nothing is anywhere or ever without its presence. Otherwise it is not at all everywhere and always powerful; and that which is not powerful everywhere and always is certainly not God. Now, if my opponent replies that it is not the divine *substance* but His *power* which is present always and everywhere, he will still not deny that God possesses His power either accidentally or substantially. But clearly God does not have power accidentally, because, while any subject can exist or be conceived apart from its accidents, God can neither be nor be conceived apart from His power. If, then, God has His power substantially, it is either part of His essence or is itself what constitutes His whole essence. It is not a part, however, because we have seen that whatever has parts can be divided either in fact or in thought; but divisibility is totally foreign to God. Therefore, the being and the power of God are one and the same. It follows, accordingly, that as the power of God exists always and everywhere, so whatever God is is present always and everywhere. Hence, when our self-styled defender of the faith says that there are three gods, he cannot show how they are separated from one another in such a way that the Father and the Holy Spirit are freed from the incarnation. In other words, positing a multiplicity of gods cannot help him to keep the Father and the spirit from being incarnate, because he cannot discover in this multiplicity of gods that distinction (*disiunctio*) which he himself argues is absolutely necessary if this freedom from incarnation is to be achieved.

VIII

However, we can easily prove that there is only one God and not several. If the two statements "God is not the highest good" and "There are several highest goods" are false, then there are not several gods but only one. Now no one denies that God is the highest good, because whatever is less than something else is certainly not God, and whatever is not the highest good is less than something else, because it is less than the highest good. And it is certain that the highest good does not allow a plurality of itself in such a way that there are several highest goods. For if there are several highest goods, they are all equal. But the highest good is that which so excels other goods that it has neither an equal nor a superior. Therefore, there is only one highest good. And this means that there are not many gods but only one God— just as there is only one highest good. The same reasoning about the highest good also applies to the highest substance, or being, or nature, and proves that it too can never be spoken of in the plural.

IX

Now, although this one and only God is three persons—Father, Son, and Holy Spirit—yet it is not necessary for the other persons to be incarnate when the Son is incarnate. On the contrary, it is impossible for them to be. For my opponent does not deny that there are several persons, since he admits that they are distinct from one another. If they were not different from one another, they would not be several. (In order to explain more briefly and easily what I want to say, I will speak, as I have done above, only of the Father and the Son, because it will thereby be clear what is to be understood of the Holy Spirit as well.) The Father and the Son, therefore, are not several or different from each other with respect to substance—for they are not two substances. The Father is not one substance and the Son another; rather, the Father and the Son are one and the same substance. However, with respect to person, they are several and different from each other—for the Father and the Son are not one and the same person, but two persons who are different from each other. My opponent says: ''If the Son was incarnate, and is not a different thing from the Father, but is numerically one and the same thing as the Father, then the Father also must have been incarnate. For it is impossible for a thing which is numerically one and the same both to be and not to be at the same time incarnate in the same man.'' To this I reply that if the Son is incarnate, and if the Son is not numerically one and the same person as the Father, but another person, then it is not necessary for the Father also to be incarnate. For it is possible for one person to be incarnate in one man and for another person not to be incarnate in this same man together with Him. But our opponent might argue: ''If God the Son is incarnate, and God who is the Son is not different from, but numerically one and the same as, God who is the Father, then even though the Father and the Son are different persons, it seems that the unity of deity would make it necessary for the Father also to be incarnate with the Son, rather than that the diversity of persons would make it possible for Him not to be incarnate together with the Son.''

Notice how he is limping on both feet regarding the incarnation of the Son of God. For whoever accepts His incarnation rightly, believes that He assumed manhood not into a unity of nature but into a unity of person. But my opponent dreams that manhood was assumed by the Son of God into a unity of nature rather than into a unity of person. For if this were not his view, he would not have said that the necessity for the Father to be incarnate with the Son (because the Father and the Son are one God) outweighs the possibility that He might not be incarnate (because of the plurality of the persons). In regard to the incarnation of the Son of God, who is one nature with the Father and another person from the Father, my opponent is therefore limping on both feet, i.e., with respect to both aspects, nature and person. Whoever considers that the incarnation refers to the unity of nature in such a way that the Son cannot be incarnate without the Father, fails to understand that the incarnation refers to the unity of person in such a way that the Father *cannot* be incarnate with the Son. Clearly God did not assume manhood in such a way that God and man were one and the same in nature, but in such a way that God and man were one and the same in person. But this assumption of manhood can only occur in respect to one person of God. For it is impossible to understand how different persons could be one and the same person in one and the same man. For if one man and several individual persons are one person, then it is necessary for several persons who are different from one another to be one and the same person—and that is impossible. Therefore, when God was incarnate with respect to any of His persons, it is impossible for Him to have been incarnate also with respect to another of the persons.

X

But why did God assume manhood into a unity of person with the Son rather than into a unity of person with either of the other persons? Since reference has now been made to this matter, I think some explanation is due, even though it was not our original intention in this letter. If the Holy Spirit [alone] had been incarnate, as the Son was incarnate, then the Holy Spirit would be the son of a human being. There would therefore be two sons in the divine Trinity, the Son of God and the son of a human being. And this would give rise to confusion when we spoke of "God the Son." For each of them would be both God and a son, even though one would be God's Son and the other a human being's. From the point of view of their being sons, there would also seem to be certain inequalities among the different persons, who ought to be wholly equal. For because of the greater dignity of His parent the one son would be superior, while the other would be subordinate because of His humbler parentage. The superiority of the Son of God to the son of a human being is exactly proportionate to the superiority of the divine Nature to human nature. Therefore, if the Holy Spirit were to be begotten of a virgin, then from the point of view of the dignity of birth one person in the Trinity would be higher and another lower, because the Son of God would have a uniquely more excellent birth (viz., from God) while the Holy Spirit would be begotten in a lesser manner (viz., from a human being). And this is not consistent [with the equality of the persons].

Further, if the *Father* were to assume manhood into a unity of person with Himself, the same incompatible plurality of sons would occur in God. And there would be an additional problem as well. For if the Father were to be the son of the Virgin, two persons in the Trinity would have the name "grandson"—the Father would be the grandson of the parents of the Virgin, and His Son would be the grandson of the Virgin, even though there would be nothing belonging to Him which originated from the Virgin. Therefore, since even a small inconsistency is impossible in God, no person of God ought to be incarnate except the Son. For nothing inconsistent follows if He is incarnate. Even when it is said that the Son is inferior to the Father and the Holy Spirit from the point of view of His humanity, this still does not mean that these two persons are superior to the Son. For that very majesty by which they are greater than the humanity of the Son belongs to the Son as well; and together with His Father and the Holy Spirit the Son Himself is superior to His own humanity.

There is also another reason why it is more fitting for the Son to be incarnate than for the other persons. He who was to be incarnate was supposed to offer prayer on behalf of the human race [i.e., one person in God was to supplicate another]. But the human mind sees it as more consistent with the relations of the persons that the Son should pray to the Father than vice versa— even though this supplication is not made by His divinity but is addressed by His humanity to divinity. The Son of God offers this prayer because through the unity of person the Son of God is a man.

Let me expand upon this somewhat. He who was going to assume manhood was sent forth to do battle against Satan and, as I have said, to intercede on behalf of man. Now when Satan and man exercised an independent (*propria*) will, they willed to make themselves like God by an act of robbery (Phil. 2:6). And because they willed by an act of robbery, they could only will unjustly, that is, only by falsehood. For the will of an angel or a man is independent when it wills contrary to the will of God. When anyone wills what God forbids, he himself is the only cause of his own willing, and his willing is therefore independently his. For, though a man sometimes submits his will to that of another man, this willing is still independent if it is in opposition to God. For he only submits it in this way to obtain something that he wants, so that he alone is the cause of his submitting his will to someone else. Therefore, [in the last analysis], an independent will is a will which is submitted to no one else. But it is the prerogative of God alone to possess such an independent will, that is, one subject to no one else.[6] And thus anyone else who exercises an independent will tries to attain to likeness with God by an act of robbery, and stands convicted of depriving God of His proper status and singular excellence, as far as it lies in him to do so. For if there is any other will which is subject to no one, the will of God will not be superior to all, nor will it be the only one which no other excels. Therefore, none of the three persons of God more fittingly "emptied Himself and took on the form of a servant" in order to conquer Satan and intercede for man (who by an act of robbery presumed to a false

6. Cf. DCD, 4.

likeness to God) than the Son. For He who is the brilliance of the
eternal light and the true image of the Father, "did not consider
it an act of robbery to be equal with God" (Phil. 2:6). But
through genuine equality and likeness He said, "I and the
Father are one" and "He who has seen me has seen the Father"
(John 10:30; 14:9). No one more justly overcomes or punishes a
criminal, or more mercifully spares him or intercedes for him,
than He to whom it is proved extraordinary injustice is done. Nor
is anything more fittingly opposed to falsehood in order to overcome it, or applied to it in order to heal it, than truth. For those
who presumed to a false likeness of God seem to have sinned
against Him who is believed to be the true likeness of God the
Father. And yet He assumed manhood into a unity of person with
Himself, as I said, in order that two natures, divine and human,
might be one person.

XI

It seems to me that there might be some value in my now
saying something about this unity of person which we most
firmly believe is in Christ, but which is not composed of two
persons. For it is possible that, if too little caution is exercised,
Christ might seem to exist from and in two persons. There are
some who ask:

Why doesn't our saying that there are two natures in Christ commit
us to saying also that there are two persons? For before the assumption of manhood God was a person, and He did not cease being a person after He assumed manhood. Moreover, the assumed man (*homo assumptus*) is a person, because every individual man is known to be a
person. This means that the person of God who existed before the incarnation is one and the person of the assumed man is another. Therefore, just as Christ is God and man, so there seems to be two persons in
Him. In other words, this reasoning appears to prove that there are
two persons in Christ, because both God and the assumed man are persons.

But this argument is not correct. For as in God one nature is a plurality of persons and the plurality of persons is one nature, so in Christ one person is a plurality of natures and the plurality of natures is one person. Just as the Father is God, the Son is God, and the Holy Spirit is God, and nevertheless there are not three gods, but one, so in Christ God is person and man is person, and nevertheless there are not two persons, but one. For, although in Christ one thing is God and another is man, this does not mean that there is one *person* who is God and another *person* who is a man. On the contrary, one and the same person is both God and man. "The Word made flesh" assumed another *nature*, not another person. When the word "man" is uttered, only the nature which is common to all men is signified. But when we say demonstratively "this man" or "that man"—or use His proper name, "Jesus"—we designate a person who, together with His nature, possesses a collection of properties by which His common humanity is individuated and by which He is differentiated from other individuals. For when He is designated in this way, not just any man at all is understood, but He to whom the angel referred in the Annunciation, He who is God and man, Son of God and Son of the Virgin, and who is whatever is truly predicated of Him according to either deity or humanity. For from the point of view of His person, it is impossible to designate or to name the Son of God apart from the son of man, and vice versa, since the same person who is the son of man is also the Son of God, and since the same collection of properties belongs both to the Word and to the assumed man. But it is impossible for the same collection of properties to belong to different persons or for these persons to be called by each other's names. Peter and Paul do not have the same collection of properties, nor is Peter called Paul, nor vice versa.

When "the Word was made flesh," therefore, He assumed the nature which alone is signified by the noun "man," and which is always different from the divine nature. He did not assume another person, because the same collection of properties as belong to the assumed man are also His. For "man" and "the man assumed by the Word," viz., Jesus, are not the same, because, as I have said, we understand by the noun "man" the nature alone, while by the assumed man or by the name "Jesus," we understand along with His nature (i.e., with His manhood) a collection of properties which is the same for both that assumed man and the Word. For this reason we do not say that the Word and "man *simpliciter*" are the same person, because we do not want to say that any and every man is the same person as the Word. On the contrary, we speak about the Word and that assumed man, viz., Jesus. In the same way, we do not believe that this man Jesus is the same person as God absolutely, but rather that He is the same person as the Word and Son. We do not believe this lest we seem to confess that this man is identical in person with the Father or the Holy Spirit. But since the Word is God and since this man assumed by the Word is man, it is true to say that God and man are the same person. However, together with the name "God" we should supply "the Word," and together with the name "man" we should understand "the Son of the Virgin."

Now, even though, except for the statement I quoted above, I have had access to nothing from the writings of the opponent to whom I am responding in this letter, I think that the truth of the matter has been made so clear by what I have said that any intelligent person will perceive that no contrary argument could be convincing.

XII

However, the alternative to a multiplicity of gods is not the denial of the plurality of persons in God. If my opponent thinks that it is, the reason must be that he does not know why this language is used of God. He has in mind not God or His persons but something like a plurality of human persons; and because he sees that it is not possible for one man to be several persons, he denies that God is several persons. But we do not speak of three persons in God because they are three separate things like three men but because they have a certain likeness (*similitudinem*) to three separate persons. Let us consider this in regard to the Father and the Son, and take it that the same can be understood also of the Holy Spirit.

Take the case of a man who is only a father and not a son, and of his son who is only a son and not a father (viz., Adam and Abel). Now we say of Adam, the father, and of Abel, the son, that the father is not a son and the son is not a father. For Adam and Abel are two men and two separate persons, and Adam is not anyone's son, and Abel is not anyone's father. In the same way, therefore, even though there are not two gods, we confess that, in God, the Father is not the Son and the Son is not the Father, because the Father does not have a father and the Son does not have a son. Similarly the Holy Spirit is not the Father or the Son, because He is not anyone's father or son. Therefore, the Father, the Son, and the Holy Spirit are three, and are distinct from one another, and their names cannot be used interchangeably (as we have shown about "father" and "son" in the above case of different human persons). This is the reason they are called three persons, not because they are three separate things.

XIII

In regard to the one God and the three persons, we thus predicate "three" of something that is one and "one" of something that is three, in such a way that the three are not predicated of one another. Now if my opponent denies that this is possible—on the ground that nothing like it is seen in other things, neither can he understand it in God—then he will have to endure the fact that there is something in God which his understanding is not able to fathom; and he will have to stop comparing a nature which is above everything, free from every law of place, time, and composition, with things which are shut up in space and time or are composed of parts. Instead, let him believe that there is something in God's nature which cannot be in created natures, and let him submit to Christian authority without arguing against it.

However, let us see whether among created things which are subject to the law of time, place, and composition we cannot to some extent find to be true that which my opponent denies to be the case in God. Suppose there is a spring from which there originates and flows a river, which later accumulates into a lake. And suppose its name is "the Nile." Now we speak of the spring, the river, and the lake separately in such a way that we would not call the spring "the river" or "the lake," nor the river "the spring" or "the lake," nor the lake "the spring" or "the river." And yet the spring is called the Nile, the river is called the Nile, and the lake is called the Nile. Similarly the spring and the river together are called the Nile, the spring and the lake together are called the Nile, and the river and the lake together are called the Nile. And the spring, the river, and the lake, all three together, are called the Nile. But yet, whether the name "Nile" is applied to them individually or in combinations of two or three, it is always one and the same Nile; there is not one Nile and another Nile. The spring, the river, and the lake, therefore, are three, and are at the same time one Nile, one stream, one nature, one water. And none of these things can be said to be three. For there are neither three Niles, streams, natures, or waters, nor three springs, rivers, or lakes. Here is an example, therefore, in which "one" is predicated of what is three and "three" of what is one, and yet the three are not predicated of one another.

Now if my opponent objects that neither the spring, the river, nor the lake singularly, nor any two of them, is the complete Nile, but only part of it, let him consider the following. The whole Nile, from where it begins to where it comes to an end, exists, as it were, through its whole lifetime. It never exists wholly and simultaneously in any time or place, but exists through its parts; and it will not be complete until it ceases to exist. For in this respect it is somewhat like speech, which, as long as it is pouring forth, as it were, from the spring of the mouth, is not complete; when it is complete, it has already come to an end. Now if anyone were to examine the matter in this way and to understand it carefully, he would realize that the whole Nile is the spring, the whole Nile is the river, and the whole Nile is the lake, and that the spring is not the river or the lake, the river is not the lake or the spring, and the lake is not the spring or the river. For the spring is not the same as the river or the lake, even though the river and the lake are what the spring is, viz., the same Nile, the same stream, the same water, the same nature. This is a case, therefore, in which "three" is predicated of one complete whole and "one complete whole" is predicated of three; and yet the three are not predicated of one another. This situation certainly exists in a very different way and more perfectly in that most simple of natures which is also completely free from every law of place and time. But yet if the above truth can be seen in some sense in something that is composite, spatial, and temporal, it is not beyond belief for it to be realized perfectly in that supremely free Nature.

We ought further to take into consideration here that the spring does not exist from the river or from the lake, while the river exists only from the spring, not from the lake, and the lake exists from both the spring and the river. This means that the whole river exists from the whole spring, and the whole lake from both the whole spring and the whole river. And this is just the way we speak about the Father, the Son, and the Holy Spirit. Moreover, there is another parallel. The river exists from the spring in one way, while the lake exists from the spring and the river in yet another way, such that the lake is not called the river. Similarly, the Son exists from the Father in His own peculiar way, while the Holy Spirit exists from the Father and the Word in another way, such that the same Holy Spirit is not the Word (or the Son), but "He Who Proceeds."

XIV

In addition, I want to mention something which, although it is quite unlike the incarnation of the Word, is yet not without some resemblance to it. It is possible, of course, that someone who reads this may think it ridiculous, but I would say that if anyone else were to put the matter like this, I would not disdain it completely. Suppose the river ran from the spring to the lake through a pipe. Then isn't it only the river which is, if I may put it this way, 'en-piped' (*infistulatus*), even though it is not a different Nile from the spring and the lake? And isn't that just like saying that only the Son is incarnate (*incarnatus*), even though He is not a different God from the Father and the Holy Spirit?

XV

But since these earthly things are far removed from the highest Nature, let us with the help of that Nature lift up our minds toward it and consider briefly some aspects of what we are saying regarding it. God is nothing other than simple eternity itself. But a plurality of eternities is unintelligible. For if there is a plurality of eternities, they are outside or inside one another. But nothing is external to eternity. Therefore, eternity is not external to eternity. Again, if they are outside one another, they exist in different places or times. But that is incompatible with eternity. There is, therefore, no plurality of eternities outside one another. But if we say that there is a plurality of eternities within one another, we ought to know that, however often eternity is repeated within eternity, only one and the same eternity is involved. And that nature which, repeated within itself, integrates with itself in perfect unity is of greater worth than one which admits plurality. Where there is plurality there is diversity; and where there is diversity there is not perfect harmony. Perfect harmony is that which integrates into one and the same unified identity. If therefore perfect harmony is better than imperfect harmony, and if it is impossible that anything imperfect should exist in the highest good (which is eternity itself), then it is not possible for the nature of eternity to admit of plurality. Hence, however often eternity is repeated within eternity, it is always one and the same unique eternity.

Now, the same kind of observation might be made about many

other things as well. For example, omnipotence within omnipotence is only one omnipotence. Or I might propose one instance of a similar situation in something which does not have a divine nature : a point within a point is only one point. For a point (such as the middle point of the world and a point of time, such as the present) has some similarity to eternity and has some value for the investigation of eternity. This question must be discussed elsewhere. Here it is sufficient to note only that a point is simple, without parts, and indivisible, like eternity, and that therefore a point added to a point makes only one point (if there is no intervening space), just as eternity added to eternity makes only one eternity.

Therefore, since God is eternity, there is no plurality of gods; for God is not external to God, and God in God does not add numerically to God. God is thus always one and the same and unique. So when God is begotten of God, since that which is begotten is not outside of the one from whom he is begotten, the offspring exists in the parent and the parent in the offspring; i.e., there is one God, who is the Father and the Son. Similarly when God proceeds from God the Father and the Son, He does not go outside of God. God [the Holy Spirit] remains in God from whom He proceeds, and there is one God—the Father, the Son, and the Holy Spirit. And because that begottenness and that procession are without beginning (since an eternity which is begotten and an eternity which proceeds cannot have a beginning), we cannot and ought not to think that God ever began to be the Father or the Son or the Holy Spirit.

XVI

However, just as the divine substance preserves its eternal and singular unity, so the nature of these relations (i.e., of the Father and the Son, or of the one who proceeds and those from whom He proceeds) retains its inseparable plurality. For it is necessary for God always to be one and the same, and not plural and different; and it is equally necessary, because of the relations of the persons, that the Father is never the same as the Son, and that He who proceeds is never the same as those from whom He proceeds. On the contrary, the Father is always other than the Son, and He who proceeds is always other than those from whom He proceeds. And these three are never spoken of interchangeably. Therefore, when God is begotten of God or when God proceeds from God, the substance cannot lose its singularity, nor the relations their plurality. The one is here three, and the three are one, and yet they are not spoken of interchangeably. And it ought not to be regarded as incredible that in a nature which is above all and is unlike anything else, something is the case of which we can find no perfect example elsewhere. (It should be noted, however, that whereas the Latins call these three persons, the Greeks call them substances.[7] For just as we say that in God there is one substance and three persons, so they say one person and three substances. But they mean by "substance" what we mean by "person," so that in faith they do not differ from us in any respect.)

Now, as regards the question how the Son is begotten of the Father, and how the Holy Spirit proceeds from the Father and the Son, and yet is not a son, we must remind ourselves that in this life it is not possible for us to see Him "as He is" (I John 3:2). The blessed Augustine has studied the matter carefully, although "through a glass darkly" (I Cor. 13:12), in his book *De Trinitate,* and I have discussed it according to my ability in the *Monologion,* which I mentioned above. Moreover, if anyone wants to know why, since there is no sexual distinction in the highest being, the parent is called Father rather than mother, and the offspring is called Son rather than daughter, or why only the Father is called Unbegotten and only the Son is called Begotten, while the Holy Spirit is called neither Begotten nor Unbegotten—he will find clear answers in that same small book of mine.

---

7. Cf. the discussion of these terms in Boethius. PL, 64:1343–1345.

On the Virgin Conception
and Original Sin
(De Conceptu Virginali
et de Originali Peccato)

PROLOGUE

Since I am willing to accommodate your religious desire on all matters in so far as I am able, brother and most beloved son Boso, I certainly count myself especially indebted when I understand that such a desire is aroused in you by me. You have read in the *Cur Deus Homo* (which you above all others urged me to write and in which I have cast you as my fellow disputant) that there is yet another argument—different from the one used in that book—which can be given to show the way in which God took from among the sinful mass of the human race a man who had no sin[1] [CDH, Bk. 2, Ch. 16]. Now, when you read this I am sure that your alert mind was in no small degree aroused to ask what the argument is. For this reason I fear that I may seem unjust to you if I conceal from you, my dear friend, what thoughts I have on this matter. So I shall briefly present my views in order that I may not reject the right opinion of anyone on this topic or stubbornly maintain my own opinion if it can be shown to be opposed to the truth. Still, I think that the argument

1. See DIV, *supra*, p. 11, n. 5.

presented in the *Cur Deus Homo* is altogether valid and sufficient if one attends to it. For nothing prevents there being
several different arguments, any one of which is sufficient to
establish the same conclusion.

Chapter I
What Original and Personal Justice
and Injustice Are

In order to see, therefore, how God assumed from out of the
sinful mass of the human race a man who had no sin, it is necessary first to inquire about original sin, because our problem
arises solely concerning this sin. For if we see how Christ could
not be subject to original sin, then it will be clear how His
assumption, or conception, was free from all sin.

There is no doubt that "original" is derived from the word
"origin." If, therefore, original sin exists only in man, it seems
to get this name either (1) from the origin, or beginning, of
human nature, on the ground that it is contracted at the very
origin of human nature, or (2) from the origin, or beginning, of
each person, on the ground that it is contracted at the very
origin of each person. However, original sin does not seem to be
something which derives from the beginning of human nature,
since human nature in its origin had justice when the first
parents were created just and without any sin. Hence, original
sin seems to be called original with respect to the origin of each
human person. Yet if anyone says this sin is called original on
the ground that individuals derive it from their first parents, in
whom human nature originated, I shall not contradict him—
provided he does not deny that original sin is contracted together with the origination of each person. Now, in each man are
found together both the *nature* by which he is a man like other
men and the *person* by which he is distinguished from other
men—as when he is called "this one" or "that one," or when he
is called by his own name (e.g., "Adam" or "Abel"). The sin of
every human being is in both his nature and his person, for the

sin of Adam was in Adam the man (i.e., in his nature) and in
the man Adam (i.e., in his person). Yet, although each man is
both a nature and a person, there is a difference between the sin
he inherits with his nature in his origin and the sin which he
does not inherit with the nature itself but which he himself
commits after he is a person distinct from other persons. That
sin which is contracted at the origin of his nature is called original, though it can also be called natural—not because it is from
the essence of his nature but because it is received together with
his nature on account of the nature's corruption. But the sin
which each man commits after he is a person can be called
personal, because it is done through a defect of the person. In a
similar manner, we can also speak both of original and of
personal justice. For Adam and Eve were originally just; that is,
in their very origin they were just, from the moment they
existed as human beings. And justice can be called personal, as
when a sinner receives justice which he did not have from his
origin.

Chapter II
How Human Nature Was Corrupted

So if Adam and Eve had kept their original justice, then those
who were born of them would likewise have been originally just.
For Adam and Eve were originally strong and uncorrupted,
having the ability always to keep justice without any difficulty.
But because they sinned personally, their whole being became
weakened and corrupt. For after sin the body was like the bodies
of brute animals—subject to corruption and carnal appetites;
and the soul was infected with carnal feelings both because of
the corruption of the body and its appetites and because of the
lack of the goods that the soul lost. And because human nature as
a whole was in Adam and Eve, and because there was no human
nature outside them, the whole human nature was weakened and
corrupted.

Therefore, along with the corruption which human nature
incurred as a result of sin, there remained in human nature both

an obligation to have the pure and perfect justice it had received and an obligation to make satisfaction for having deserted this justice. Accordingly, as human nature if it had not sinned would have reproduced itself in the form in which it was created by God [i.e., without corruption], so, having sinned, it reproduces itself in its corrupted form. So, since human nature is unable by itself either to make satisfaction for sin or to recover its deserted justice and since "the body which is corrupted burdens the soul" (Wisd. of Sol. 9:15), so that the soul is not able even to understand justice (especially when the soul is rather weak, as in infancy or in the mother's womb), it seems necessary for the human nature which is born in infants to have both the obligation to make satisfaction for that first sin which it was always able to avoid and the obligation to have that original justice it was always able to keep. Nor, in infants, is human nature's inability to discharge these obligations any excuse, for human nature brought this inability upon itself when it deserted justice in our first parents. Human nature was complete in our first parents, and so it is always under the obligation to have the ability which it received for the sake of always keeping justice. This inability can be considered to constitute original sin in infants.

Let me also mention the sins of our recent ancestors which are reckoned "unto the third and fourth generation" (Ex. 20:5). For, although one may inquire whether or not such sins are to be understood as part of original sin, I would not wish to appear to be lightening the seriousness of original sin on account of these. So I shall regard original sin to be of such gravity that no one can show it to be even more grievous.

CHAPTER III
THAT SIN EXISTS ONLY IN A RATIONAL WILL

However, whether original sin consists of all the above [viz., the inability of nature and the sins of recent ancestors] or whether it is something less, I think that original sin can in no way be asserted to be in an infant before he has a rational soul, any more than justice can be asserted to have been in Adam before he was a rational man. And if Adam and Eve had begotten offspring before they sinned, justice still would not and could not have been in the seed until it was formed into a living man. If, therefore, the seed of a man is not capable of receiving justice before it becomes a man, then the seed is also not able to receive original sin before it becomes a man.

Certainly we should not doubt that original sin is injustice. For if every sin is injustice, and if original sin is a sin, then original sin is injustice. However, if someone says that not every sin is injustice, then he should also assert that it is possible for there to be a certain sin in someone and yet, at the same time, no injustice. But such an assertion is incredible. Moreover, someone may say that original sin is not an unqualified sin; and he may argue that the words ''original sin'' are to be understood like the expression ''depicted man'' [a portrait]; for a depicted man is not really a man but only a depicted man. But from this argument it would immediately follow that an infant, who has only original sin, is free from sin; and then the Son of the Virgin[2] would not be the only man who was without sin both in His mother's womb and at His birth. If this were the case, then either those infants who have only original sin and die without baptism would not be condemned, or else they would be condemned without sin. But we accept neither of these alternatives. So we must conclude that every sin is injustice and that since original sin is an unconditional sin it is also injustice. Or, again, if God condemns a man only because of his injustice, and if He condemns someone because of original sin, then it follows that original sin is nothing other than injustice. But if this is true, and if injustice is nothing other than the absence of required justice (for injustice seems to be only in a nature which does not

2. It is clear from DP, 9 (S–203:16–17(II)), that ''*filius virginis*'' refers to the Son of Mary. Hence, it is best translated ''the Son of the Virgin''— thus uniquely characterizing Jesus. In DCV, 13, 19, however, Anselm takes up the general case of ''a man born of a virgin.'' The context suffices to indicate that ''*filius virginis*'' is no longer being used as a unique description—so that now the indefinite article is appropriate.

have justice though it ought to), then original sin is clearly included in the definition of "injustice."

But if justice is "uprightness of will kept for its own sake," and if uprightness can only be in a rational nature, then even as no nature except a rational nature can receive justice, so no nature except a rational nature is under obligation to justice. For this reason, since there can be injustice only where there ought to be justice, original sin—which is injustice—can be only in a rational nature. Now, rational nature exists only in God, in angels, and in that soul with respect to which a man is said to be rational and without which he is not a man. And since there is no original sin in God or the angels, original sin exists only in man's rational soul.

We must also realize that if justice is uprightness of will kept for its own sake, then justice can be only in the will; and only the will can have injustice. For the absence of justice is called injustice only where there ought to be justice. Hence, nothing is said to be just or unjust except (1) justice itself or injustice, (2) the will, or (3) something depending on a just or unjust will. And we call men, angels, the soul, and the soul's actions either just or unjust solely with respect to the will.

CHAPTER IV
THAT NOTHING IS JUST OR UNJUST IN ITSELF EXCEPT JUSTICE ITSELF OR INJUSTICE; AND THAT NOTHING IS PUNISHED EXCEPT THE WILL

Nothing whatsoever—whether a substance or an action or anything else—is considered to be just in itself except justice, or considered to be unjust or sinful except injustice. This applies even to the will itself, in which justice and injustice exist. For the will and justice are not identical. The former is that power of soul by which the soul wills something, and which can be called the instrument of willing, even as sight is called the instrument of seeing. And the latter is that whose possession makes the will just and whose absence makes the will unjust. Moreover, the affections and uses of this instrument are also called wills, but it would take too long to enumerate them here.[3]

Not even those appetites which the Apostle calls both "the flesh which lusts against the spirit" and "the law of sin which is in our members, warring against the law of our mind" (Gal. 5:17; Rom. 7:25), are just or unjust considered in themselves. For in themselves they do not make a man who feels them either just or unjust, but they make him unjust only if he consents to them by an act of will when he ought not. For the same Apostle says, "There is no condemnation to them who are in Christ Jesus, who walk not after the flesh" (Rom. 8:1)—that is, to those who do not give willing consent to the flesh. For if having these appetites, even without consenting to them, constitutes injustice, then a man would be condemned merely for having them. And so we see that it is not sin to have these appetites, but is only sin to consent to them [when one ought not]. Moreover, if the appetites were intrinsically unjust, then every case of consenting to them would constitute injustice. But irrational animals are not called unjust when they consent to them. Or, again, if the appetites were sins, they would be removed by baptism, which washes away every sin.[4] But this clearly does not occur. Therefore, there is no injustice in the essence of the appetites, but only in a rational will which complies with them inordinately. For when the will resists them by delighting in the law of God according to the inward man, then the will is just. For the Apostle calls the justice which the law commands "the law of God," because it is from God; and he also calls justice "the law of the mind," because it is known by the mind—just as the old law is called "the law of God," because it is from God, and also called "the law of Moses," because it was made known through Moses.

I have said that no action is to be called unjust in itself, but only on account of an unjust will. This is plain in the case of certain acts which can be done at times and not be unjust—for

3. This elaboration comes in DC, III, 11.
4. Cf. DC, III, 8.

example, killing a man (as Phinehas did) or sexual intercourse (as within marriage or among irrational animals). But there are other actions whose injustice seems more difficult to ascribe simply to an unjust will, inasmuch as they are always unjust— for example, perjury and certain other things which ought not be named. Now, consider a certain sinful action which exists only while it is doing something and which ceases after it has accomplished this thing; or consider a sinful work which has been done and which remains after the act of doing it has ceased. (For example, when someone writes something which he ought not, the writing remains even after the act of writing it has ceased.) If it were the case that an action were sinful in itself, then when the action ceased and no longer existed sin also would cease; or if it were the case that a work were sinful in itself, then as long as the work remained sin also would remain. But we see that sins are often not eliminated even when sinful actions are eliminated, and we see that sins are sometimes eliminated even when sinful works are not eliminated. For this reason, neither an action which ceases nor a work which remains is ever sin in itself.

Finally, if our members and our senses are blamed for their execution of voluntary actions, then they can reply: "God subjected us and the power that is in us to the will, so that we cannot keep from moving ourselves when the will commands, and so that we cannot keep from doing what it wills. Indeed, the will moves us as if we were its instruments, and *it* does the works which we seem to do. We cannot resist it by our own strength, nor can the works which it does be prevented by us. And neither can we nor ought we refuse to obey the will, for God has appointed it to be our master. When we obey the will, we are obeying God, who ordained this law for us." Therefore, how can the members or the senses or their works (all of which God has subjected to the will) be sinful if they observe that order which God has ordained for them? So, then, whatever the members and senses do must all be imputed to the will.

Since the actions of the members and senses are imputed to the will, someone may wonder why the members and the senses are punished for the fault of the will. But in fact only the will is punished and not the members and the senses. For nothing is punishment for anyone except that which is against his will (that is, whatever he does not want), and only a being who has a will can experience punishment. But the members and the senses will nothing through themselves. Thus, just as the will acts through the members and the senses, so it is also tormented or delighted through them. If anyone objects to this statement, then let him recall that it is really the soul (to which the will belongs) which feels and acts in those senses and members and which is tormented or delighted in them. We are accustomed to say that the actions done by an unjust will are sins, because sin exists in the will which does them. Moreover, names such as "fornication" or "lying" are given to certain actions in order to signify that they are done unjustly. But one thing is understood when we consider an action or an utterance in itself, and another when we consider whether it is done justly or unjustly. Finally, every being is from God, from whom nothing unjust proceeds. Therefore, no being is unjust in itself.

CHAPTER V
THAT THE EVIL WHICH IS SIN OR INJUSTICE IS NOTHING

Like blindness, injustice is nothing at all. For blindness is nothing other than the absence of sight where sight ought to be; and the absence of sight is nothing more in an eye, where sight ought to be, than it is in a piece of wood, where sight ought not to be. For injustice is not a definite thing which is able to infect and corrupt the soul in the same way that poison infects and corrupts the body, nor can it do something in the same way that a wicked man does evil deeds. When a savage beast, having broken its bonds, rages about wildly, we say that this is caused by the absence of chains—not because the absence of chains is anything or causes something, but because chains would have

kept the beast from raging. Or, again, if a helmsman, having left
the rudder, delivers his ship to the wind and the waves, so that it
is tossed and driven into every kind of danger, we say that the
lack of a rudder causes this—not because the lack of a rudder is
or causes anything, but because a rudder would have kept the
ship from danger.[5] So, too, when an evil man rages and is driven
into those evil deeds which are a danger to his soul, we say that
injustice causes these actions—not because injustice has being or
causes anything, but because justice would have kept them from
happening. For when justice is absent from the will, to which all
the voluntary motions of the whole man are subordinated, then
the will is without a helmsman and is uncontrolled and tossed
about. In such a state it is driven by various appetites until it
precipitates itself and all the members subordinated to it into
manifold evils. But if justice had been present in the will, it
would have kept all this from happening.

Therefore, even though the affections and acts of an unjust
will are usually called injustice, and even though they are
something when considered in themselves, we can easily see that
injustice itself has no being. And, for the same reason, we understand evil to be nothing. For as injustice is nothing other than
the absence of a required justice, so evil is nothing other
than the absence of a required good. No being, however evil it is
said to be, is nothing; but for it to be evil is not for it to be
something. For a being to be evil is simply for it to lack a good
which it ought to have; and for it to lack a good which it ought
to have is not for it to be something. Therefore, for any being to
be evil is not for it to be something.

I have been discussing briefly that evil which is injustice and
which is undoubtedly nothing at all. There is, of course, another
kind of evil, namely, the evil of disadvantage—for disadvantages
are called evil. Sometimes these disadvantages are nothing (e.g.,
blindness and deafness) and sometimes they seem to be something (e.g., grief and sadness). But I think I have sufficiently
shown in *The Fall of Satan* that justice is uprightness of will
kept for its own sake, that injustice has no being since it is only

5. Cf. DCD, 26, where the same example is used.

the absence of a required justice, that every being is from God, and that nothing comes from God except what is good. Moreover, I have discussed the notion of justice still more fully in the dialogue *Concerning Truth*.

CHAPTER VI
THAT NEVERTHELESS WHEN GOD PUNISHES A MAN FOR SIN HE DOES NOT PUNISH HIM FOR NOTHING

There are certain people who, when they hear that sin is nothing, are accustomed to ask, "If sin is nothing, then why does God punish a man for sin—for no one should be punished for nothing?" Although this is a lowly question, some kind of answer should be given to them because they do not really understand what they are asking.

Now, although it is true that the absence of justice is nothing both where there ought to be justice and where it ought not to be, yet God rightly punishes sinners on account of something and not on account of nothing. For, as I have shown in the *Cur Deus Homo*, God both exacts from recalcitrant sinners the honor due to Him which they were unwilling to repay freely and He separates these sinners from just persons by an appropriate arrangement so that nothing disordered might exist in His kingdom. [Thus God punishes for something and not for nothing.] Yet, God does not punish for their lack of justice (i.e., on account of nothing) creatures in whom justice ought not to be; for justice is not something that He should demand of them, nor is it required by the harmonious order of the universe. Thus, when God punishes a man for sin (which is the absence of justice and hence is nothing), He does not punish him on account of nothing at all. And since it is true that God does not punish a man unless there is something on account of which He should punish him, then God does not punish at all for nothing.

CHAPTER VII

HOW THE SEED OF MAN
IS SAID TO BE UNCLEAN
AND TO BE CONCEIVED IN SIN,
EVEN THOUGH THERE BE NO SIN IN IT

I think the following things, which we have already discussed, are clear: (1) that sin and injustice are nothing; (2) that they exist only in a rational will; and (3) that only the will can properly be called unjust. So it seems to follow either that from the very moment of his conception an infant has a rational soul (without which he cannot have a rational will) or else that at the moment of his conception he has no original sin. But no sensible person thinks that an infant has a rational soul from the very moment of his conception. For from such a view it would follow that whenever the human seed which has been received perishes before attaining a human form[6] (even should it perish at the moment of its reception), then the [alleged] human soul in that seed would be condemned, since it would not have been reconciled to God in Christ. But such a conclusion is utterly absurd. And so the supposition that an infant has a rational soul at the very moment of his conception must be given up.

But if the infant does not have sin from the moment of his conception, then why does Job say to God: "Who can make a man clean from an unclean seed except Thou alone?" (Job 14:4). And how is David's statement true when he says: "I was begotten in iniquity, and in sin did my mother conceive me" (Ps. 51:5)? Thus, in so far as I am able I shall inquire how infants are said to be conceived in iniquity and sin, and to be conceived from unclean seed even though there is no sin in them at the moment of their conception.

Now, Holy Scripture often asserts that something is already

6. "*Humanam figuram.*"

the case, not because it really is already the case but because it is certain that it is going to happen. Thus, with respect to the forbidden tree, God said to Adam: "In the day that you eat of it, you shall surely die" (Gen. 2:17). But this did not mean that on that day Adam's body would actually die, but only that on that day it would become necessary for Adam to be going to die. And Paul also speaks concerning the necessity of dying some-day: "But if Christ be in you, the body is dead because of sin; but the spirit is alive because of justification" (Rom. 8:10). But this was not spoken to those whose bodies were already dead, but to those whose bodies were going to die on account of sin, since "Through one man sin entered into the world, and through sin came death" (Rom. 5:12). Thus, when Adam sinned we all sinned in him—not because we sinned before we even existed, but because we were going to be born from Adam and because it became necessary at that time that we would be going to sin when we existed. For "through one man's disobedience, many men were sinners" (Rom. 5:19).

In the same way, man can be understood to be conceived in iniquity and sin, and from unclean seed—not because there is actually any iniquity, sin, or uncleanness in the seed itself, but because from that seed and its conception there occurs the necessity that man will have the uncleanness of sin (uncleanness *is* sin and iniquity) just as soon as he has a rational soul. For even if an infant is begotten by means of a corrupt concupis-cence, there is no more guilt in the seed than there is in the spittle spat forth by means of the evil will of an angry man, or even in the shedding of his own blood. For what is at fault is not the spittle or the blood but the evil will. So it is clear how it can be true that there is no sin in infants at the time of their concep-tion and how Holy Scripture can appear to oppose this. For there is no sin in infants at that moment, since there is no will in them; nevertheless, sin can be said to be in them because they contract in the seed the necessity of sinning as soon as they are human beings.

CHAPTER VIII
THAT THERE IS NEITHER SIN
NOR THE NECESSITY OF FUTURE SIN
IN THE SEED ASSUMED FROM THE VIRGIN

Now if I am right, then the seed which is taken from the parent has no sin in it, because it does not yet have a will. So it is clear that what the Son of God assumed from the Virgin into His person could not have been blemished by sin. But we have said that the seed is contracted from parents with the necessity of sinning at that future time when it will have been enlivened with a rational soul. There are only three reasons for this necessity of sinning. First, human nature is born in infants with the obligation to make satisfaction for the sin of Adam (and, according to what I have said, for the sins of its recent ancestors). Yet human nature cannot make satisfaction; and as long as it does not, it sins. Second, human nature cannot recover by means of its own efforts the justice which it has deserted. And, third, the soul is weighed down by a corrupted body and cannot even understand justice; but if the soul cannot understand justice, then it can neither have it nor keep it. Therefore, if it can be shown that the seed which the Son of God assumed from the Virgin is free from these three necessities, then it will be clear that it contracted no necessity of sinning.

Now, if we eliminate from the seed of the Virgin the first necessity (through which it would seem to be obliged to make satisfaction for the sins of its first and recent ancestors), then from a consideration of the personal unity of the one who assumes and the nature which is assumed, it will be easy to show that this seed is also free from the second and third necessities. (The second necessity is that according to which human nature cannot by itself alone recover justice. And the third necessity is that by which the corrupted body weighs down the soul, so that without the help of grace the soul is unable to keep the justice which is received at the perfect age,[7] and so that the soul of infants is unable even to understand what justice is.) And if it can be shown that the seed which descends from Jesus' first parents is free from the obligation of making satisfaction for sin, then without a doubt no such obligation can descend to Him from His more recent ancestors. So with the help of God I shall try to show how the seed which descends from Jesus' first parents is free from the necessity of making satisfaction for sin—though, since this has already been shown in other words, it is not necessary to discuss it here at great length.

CHAPTER IX

WHY THE SIN BY WHICH THE HUMAN RACE IS CONDEMNED IS IMPUTED TO ADAM RATHER THAN TO EVE, EVEN THOUGH ADAM SINNED AFTER EVE AND ON HER ACCOUNT

It seems to me that we should first ask why the sin by which the human race is condemned is more often and more particularly imputed to Adam than to Eve, although she sinned before Adam did and he sinned because of her. For the Apostle says, "But death reigned from Adam until Moses, even over those who did not sin in the likeness of Adam's transgression" (Rom. 5:14). And there are many other texts which seem to incriminate Adam more than Eve.

I think Scripture speaks this way because a union of two things often takes its name from the chief member of the union, just as a whole often takes its name from one of its parts. Or Scripture may speak this way because the name "Adam" was applicable both to Adam and to his rib, although his rib was fashioned into a woman—just as we read that God "created them male and female, and blessed them, and called their name 'Adam' on the day in which they were created" (Gen. 5:2). Or, again, Scripture may speak this way because if only Eve had

7. "*In aetate perfecta.*"

sinned, but not Adam, it would not have been necessary for the whole human race to perish, but only for Eve to perish. For from Adam, in whom the seed of all mankind had been created, God could have made another woman through whom His purpose with respect to Adam might have been accomplished. For these same reasons, I shall refer to these two people by the one name "Adam"—except in those places where it is necessary to distinguish between them.

CHAPTER X
WHY MEN WHO WERE NOT CONSCIOUS OF ADAM'S SIN ARE WEIGHED DOWN BY IT

Each of us, being a son of Adam, is a man by virtue of creation; and each of us is Adam by virtue of propagation; and each of us is a person by virtue of the individuation by which we are distinguished from one another. For we do not have our manhood from Adam, but through him. Just as Adam did not cause his own manhood, so he did not create in himself this human nature which can reproduce. Rather God, who created him a man, created in him that nature by which he might propagate other men. Therefore, we need have no doubt why each of us is under the obligation we have been discussing. We are not under this obligation because we are men or because we are persons: For if anyone were liable for this debt simply because he is a man or is a person, then it would have been necessary for Adam himself to have been under this obligation even before he sinned —since he was even then a man and a person. But such a consequence is completely absurd. So the remaining alternative is that man is a debtor only in so far as he is Adam. But he is not a debtor simply because he is Adam, but because he is Adam the Sinner. For if he were a debtor simply because he is Adam, then it would follow that even if Adam himself had not sinned, those who are propagated from him would still have been born with this debt. But such a thought is impious.

It is not out of place here to repeat the question which was

asked above, namely, why someone who was not conscious of
Adam's sin should be nonetheless weighed down by Adam's sin
or debt simply because of being propagated from him. When God
created Adam He made in him a reproductive nature; and God
subjected this nature to Adam's power, so that Adam might use
it in accordance with his own will as long as he willingly submitted to God. But his reproductive nature was not meant to be
used for irrational bestial pleasure, but rather in accordance
with a rational human will. For just as it is characteristic of
beasts to will nothing rationally, so it is proper to men to will
nothing apart from reason. For men should always will in
accordance with reason, because Adam received from God, and
could always have kept, the power to will in accordance with
reason. When God created Adam directly, without the working
of any reproductive nature and apart from the will of any
creature, He made Adam rational and just. And God also gave
Adam grace such that, if he had not sinned, those whom he
would beget by his will and by the working of his nature would
also be just in the moment they had rational souls.

The argument presented in the *Cur Deus Homo* to show that
rational nature was created just also shows that if Adam had not
sinned, then those propagated from this human nature would
necessarily have received justice along with rationality. For God,
who created the first man other than by means of parental generation, also creates those who are propagated through the first
man's created nature. So if Adam had not sinned, then every
man would have been rational and just at the same time—even
as he was. But since Adam was unwilling to be subject to the will
of God, his reproductive nature (which remained in him) was no
longer subject to his will as it would have been if he had not
sinned. So he lost the grace which he could have kept for those
who were going to be propagated from him; and all who are
propagated by the working of the nature which Adam received
are born under his obligation to make satisfaction. For human
nature as a whole was in Adam, and no part of it was in anyone
else; and by sinning without any necessity, human nature dishonored God and could not make any satisfaction to God by

itself. Therefore, Adam lost that grace which he received and which he could always have kept on behalf of those who were going to be propagated from him; and for these descendants he also contracted sin and its accompanying penalty—in so far as sin and its penalty are propagated in his descendants through the reproductive nature which was given to him.

Chapter XI
That Propagation from the Virgin Is Not Subject to the Law and the Merits of Natural Propagation; and That There Are Three Courses of Things

Now we must carefully consider whether or not this so-called inheritance of sin and of the penalty of sin is justly transmitted to the man who was propagated from Adam through the Virgin. Indeed, it is certain that the reproductive nature which Adam received works only through the conjunction of a man and a woman. For it is not within the power of human nature, and it is known to be impossible, that a man alone or a woman alone—simply by the working of his own nature and will—could beget offspring. For just as the clay of the earth had not received a nature or a will by which to produce the first man (although the clay was that from which the first man was able to be made by God), so also a woman was not made from the rib of Adam, nor was a man made from a woman alone, by the working of human nature and will. Rather, God, by His own power and will, made one man from clay, made another man from a woman alone, and made a woman from a man alone. For, although nothing is done except by the efficient or permitting will of God, nevertheless certain things are done by His power and will alone, certain other things are done by the created nature, and still other things by the will of the creature. But just as created nature can do nothing of itself except what it has received from the will of

God, so the will of the creature cannot do anything by itself except what created nature assists in or concedes to. For in the beginning the will of God alone made the natures of things, giving to some of them wills appropriate to their nature, so that these natures and these wills might perform their work in the course of things in accordance with that order which God prescribed for them. Moreover, God does many other things by means of the working of these natures and wills, which they could not at all have done in accordance with their appointed use and purpose.

For when the sea offers a dry path within itself to a people, or when the dead rise, or when water is suddenly changed into wine, or when the hearts of men are taught by the Holy Spirit certain things which they do not know either from themselves or from another creature, or when by the directing of grace alone evil wills are converted from their own impulses unto that which is beneficial, and when many other things are done which neither the creature nor its will might have done through its own accustomed course of activity—these things are the work of God's will alone. Nature draws what is heavy downward and what is light upward. Nature makes the earth bring forth countless plants and trees, and makes these bear fruit—and sometimes she does this by first using a human will which plants and cultivates the earth, and other times she does this without any working of a human will. And we know, more from experience than from what we are taught, that nature does many other such works. But things such as traveling, building, writing, speaking, and the like, are attributed to the will rather than to nature; for the will alone causes such things as these.

Therefore, if we carefully consider all the things which are done, we see that they occur either by the will of God alone, or by nature according to the power given to it by God, or by the will of a creature. Now, those things which are not done by created nature or by the will of a creature, but done by God alone, are miracles. Thus, it appears that there are three courses of things, viz., the miraculous, the natural, and the voluntary. And indeed the miraculous is not subject to the other two or to their laws,

but it freely rules over them; nor does it do violence to them
when it seems to oppose them, since they have nothing except
what they received from the miraculous, and all that they have
received is under it. Therefore, like the propagation which
brought forth a woman from a man alone, and like the creation
of a man from clay, the propagation of a man from a virgin
alone is neither natural nor voluntary, but miraculous. For this
reason it is clear that the propagation from the Virgin is not at
all subject to the laws and merits of that propagation which the
will and nature (each in its own way) collaborate in effecting.
For in this collaboration the will does one thing and nature does
another. Nevertheless, just as any man or woman who exists
from the union of a man and a woman is truly man—so Adam,
who existed from no other man, is truly man, and so Jesus, who
existed from a woman alone, is truly man, and so Eve, who
existed from a man alone, is truly man. Moreover, every man is
either Adam or from Adam; but Eve is from Adam alone, and
all others are from Adam and Eve. Because Mary, from whom
alone Jesus exists, is from Adam and Eve, it follows that He
Himself must be from the same pair. For it was expedient that
He who was going to redeem the human race should exist and be
born from the father and mother of all men.

Chapter XII
That It Is Not Right for Adam's Evils to Be Passed to That Man

It is also easy to understand why the Son of the Virgin could
not be subject to the sin, or debt, of Adam. For Adam was
created just: he was free from sin, its often-mentioned debt, and
its penalty. And Adam was created happy and with the ability to
keep forever the justice he had received; and through his keeping justice he was able to keep the freedom and happiness I have
just mentioned. Since he did not keep these goods for himself
(although he was always able to do so without any difficulty), he
removed them from himself and subjected himself to their

opposite. And Adam was made the servant of sin, or injustice, and the servant of a debt which he was unable to repay, and the servant of that wretchedness which is characterized by the inability to recover the goods which he had lost. Just as he was unable to remove from himself the goods which he had (or to bring upon himself the evils which he did not have) in any other way than by not keeping those goods for himself when he could have, so he was only able to remove those goods from others (and only able to bring those evils upon others) by not keeping those goods for the persons for whom he was able to keep them. But Adam was able to keep those goods for no one except for those persons whose possibility of generation had been made subject to his will. Hence, Adam could not transmit the aforementioned evils to any person (even though propagated from him) unless either Adam's reproductive nature or Adam's will worked or was able to work something in the generation of that person. Therefore, by no right or reason can it be shown that these evils of Adam pass down to the man conceived by the Virgin.

CHAPTER XIII
THAT EVEN IF SUCH A MAN WERE NOT GOD, BUT ONLY AND ENTIRELY A MAN, IT WOULD STILL BE NECESSARY FOR HIM TO BE AS THE FIRST MAN WAS CREATED TO BE

Or, again, if we carefully examine the wise justice of God with the pure gaze of reason, then we recognize that it is completely absurd that Adam's sin, or debt, or penalty should be transmitted to a man born of a virgin. And this would be the case even if such a man were not assumed into the person of God but were only and entirely a man. For it is absurd that Adam's sin, debt, and penalty should be passed down through a seed which is produced solely by the will of God—a seed which is not produced or brought forth by any created nature, or by the will of any creature, or by a power given by God to anyone else; for in order to beget a man by means of a new power, God takes from a virgin this seed which is free from sin. In this case a rational mind understands that for the same reason that God ought to create Adam fully just and unburdened by any debt or disadvantage, so a man who is begotten by God's own will and power ought to be created free from subjection to any evil. For it would be utterly repugnant to God's omnipotent and wise goodness for Him to make—by His own will alone and from matter (in which there is no sin)—a rational nature which was subjected to evil. Whoever does not understand this fact does not know what is unfitting with respect to God. Therefore, even if God thus produced a mere man (as I said above), it would still be necessary for God to endow him with no less justice and happiness than Adam possessed when he was first created.

CHAPTER XIV
THAT WHAT IS WRITTEN—"MAN IS CONCEIVED FROM UNCLEAN SEED AND IN INIQUITY" —DOES NOT OPPOSE THE PROPOSED ARGUMENT, EVEN THOUGH THESE TEXTS MAY APPLY PROPERLY IN SOME CASES

Perhaps someone may not understand the things which I have said regarding the seed of man, namely, that there is no sin in it before it becomes a rational soul, and that this seed is called unclean in sin and iniquity on account of a later uncleanness which will be in man. And perhaps someone may think that the seed is unclean in the moment of its conception because he reads the two verses which I have already opposed to my own argument—namely, "Who can make a man clean from an unclean seed?" and "I was begotten in iniquity, and in sin did my mother conceive me" (Job 14:4; Ps. 51:5). If there is any such person, there is no need for me to strive here to make him understand what he cannot understand; but I ask him now to listen closely to a few things which I am going to say.

Surely those who have written these Scripture verses either wanted them to be understood as referring to the seed of every man or else as referring only to that seed which is inseminated with the sense of pleasure which would have been proper only to irrational animals had man not sinned. But if such great men meant this text to refer to all men, then they would have been affirming that the seed taken from the Virgin alone would also be unclean—something blasphemous to believe. Therefore, they were not writing about that seed. But if they spoke of a man's seed in the other sense, then they wanted this uncleanness understood only of the seed which is conceived with the pleasure just mentioned. But this alternative is in no way opposed to our argument, which asserts that the seed taken from the Virgin is clean even though it be from the sinful mass.

CHAPTER XV
HOW THE SINFUL MASS IS NOT TOTALLY SINFUL

Blindness is not in every part of a man when he is called blind (for it is only in his eyes, where there ought to be sight, and not in his hands or in his feet). In the same way, the deafness of a man who is called deaf is only in his ears. Similarly, although the mass of the human race is called sinful, sin is not in every part but only in the will, which does not exist in the seed at the time of the conception of any man. Therefore, if we consider these things, we see that neither true nor apparent reasons contradict them. So we can now freely conclude that there is no reason, no truth, or no understanding which allows us to assert that anything pertaining to the sin of the sinful mass could or should have affected that man who was conceived from the Virgin alone. And this conclusion is true, even though He was assumed from that sinful mass; and it would still be true even if He were not God.

Chapter XVI

Why John the Baptist and Others Who Were Also Conceived by Miracle Are Not as Such Free from Sin

But someone may object that John the Baptist and certain other men were begotten from sterile parents and from parents in whom the reproductive nature was already dead because of old age; and they may pursue our line of argument and say that these men also ought to have been born without sin and its penalty because they too were conceived by a miracle. But such people should understand that there is a very different reason which shows that the virgin conception is necessarily free from all sin. For it is one thing for God to heal a nature which is enfeebled by old age or by some defect and to recall it to its proper working; but it is another thing for God to cause something to occur which is not only unheard of but even unimaginable and unknown to nature. For if Adam had not sinned, then not only would he have remained unweakened by old age or any other infirmity, but also that nature created in him for the sake of reproduction would not have been impeded from its natural course by any mishap; and its use would have remained subject to his power. Therefore, while in the case of the Son of the Virgin something new was given with respect to Adamic nature, nothing new was given in the case of John and others like him; but we know that their nature, which was weakened as a result of its own work, is simply restored. Therefore, since all these men were begotten by means of that natural propagation which was given to Adam, they neither can nor ought to be likened unto Jesus, whose miraculous conception we have been discussing; hence, they cannot be shown to be free from the bond of original sin.

CHAPTER XVII
WHY GOD WAS INCARNATED EVEN THOUGH HE WAS ABLE TO MAKE FROM ADAM AS MANY SINLESS BUT SIMPLY HUMAN MEN AS WERE SUFFICIENT [TO COMPLETE THE HEAVENLY CITY]

Now, perhaps someone will say: "If, as you maintain, someone who was purely man (and not God) could be made from Adam without any taint of sin, then why was it necessary for God to be incarnated? For either God was able to redeem sinners through one such man who was without any sin or else by means of a similar kind of miracle God was able to make as many men as were necessary to complete the Heavenly City."

I shall briefly reply to this. First, God was made man because a man who was not God [*homo non-deus*] would not have been sufficient for the redemption of other men—as I pointed out in the oft-cited *Cur Deus Homo*. And, second, God did not, by means of a miracle, make as many men as were necessary to fill up the Heavenly City lest (if none of those who were propagated by natural means were saved) it should seem that He had created human nature in Adam in vain and later corrected it, as if He had not made it properly in the first place. But it is not fitting for Supreme Wisdom first to make and later to correct any nature.

Now, you remember that I proposed above to inquire how that seed which was taken from the Virgin and in which we have seen that there was no sin, could be free from those three necessities in which all men are conceived. I was confident that if it could first be shown rationally that this seed was free from the necessity of making satisfaction for the sin of Adam and of recent ancestors, then—because the man Jesus is God—His seed could also be free from the other two necessities; viz., from that necessity by which human nature is unable by itself to recover the justice it has deserted and from that necessity by which "the body which is corrupted weighs down the soul" (especially the souls of infants). I began by asking how we should understand the reason for Jesus' freedom from the necessity of making satisfaction for Adam's sin. I did this so that afterwards it would be easier to find what I sought with respect to the other two necessities. And by the abundant grace of that one whose sinless conception we are discussing, it happened that not only did we see that the seed of Jesus was free from all the aforesaid necessities of sin and debt, but we also rationally proved that a man thus conceived ought to be endowed with no less justice and happiness than Adam was endowed with when he was created. And this should be the case even if a man thus conceived were not God, but were only and entirely man. For indeed it seemed irrational both that (1) sin or the penalty of sin should descend from any ancestors to one born by means of such a propagation and (2) that God should freely create an unjust rational nature or that He should make a rational nature wretched when there is no injustice in it which merits wretchedness.

Chapter XVIII

That God Was Not Conceived from a Just Virgin by Necessity—as If He Could Not Have Been Conceived from a Sinful Virgin—but He Was Conceived in This Way Because It Was Fitting

Although it is absolutely true that the Son of God was conceived from a most pure virgin, nevertheless this was not done by necessity—as if it were rationally impossible for a just offspring to be begotten from a sinful parent through this kind of propagation. But it was done because it was fitting that this man should be conceived from a most pure mother. For, since God the Father was disposed to give the Virgin His only Son (whom from His own heart He begot as equal to Himself and loved as much as Himself) so that He would naturally be the common son of God the Father and the Virgin, and since the Son Himself chose to make her substantially His mother, and since the Holy Spirit willed and was going to cause the Son from whom He proceeded to be conceived and born from her, then it was fitting that the Virgin should be radiant with a purity so great that a greater purity cannot be conceived (other than the purity of God Himself). And I have already discussed [in the *Cur Deus Homo*] how the Virgin was made sinless by means of faith before that conception; however, in that writing I presented another argument concerning this point.

CHAPTER XIX

HOW THIS ARGUMENT AND THE ONE IN THE *Cur Deus Homo* ARE ALIKE, AND HOW THEY ARE DIFFERENT

Either of these two arguments seems to be sufficient in itself to handle this one question; but jointly they fully satisfy a mind that is seeking both an argument which is sound and an event which is fitting. For, although the argument there and the one here move toward the same conclusion, they differ in the following respect: The one I have given in this treatise shows that, by means of a virgin conception, God should produce a just man (and only a just man) from the substance of a virgin *even if* she were sinful—for sin is nowhere in the nature of man except in the will. And the other argument shows that even if sin pervaded the essence of a virgin, nevertheless by means of faith this virgin would be able to become free from sin (in regard to the sinlessness of such a conception). And in the argument I have presented in this treatise, all necessity of death, travail, and corruption of every kind is clearly excluded from the man born of the Virgin; but in the *Cur Deus Homo* a question concerning His necessity of dying seems to arise—though if someone closely examines the argument there he will see that it is sufficient to solve this question. And so from these two arguments we see clearly that it was only because of His holy will [and not because of any necessity] that our Lord and Redeemer took upon Himself all the things which He suffered.

CHAPTER XX

THAT HE WHO WAS BORN OF THE VIRGIN HAD ORIGINAL JUSTICE IN PLACE OF ORIGINAL SIN

Now, I think that I have adequately shown what I set out to prove concerning original sin, namely, how from His ancestors it could in no way be transmitted to the man conceived from the Virgin. And I have shown that reason requires that He ought rather to be created happy and just. Since from His very origin, as we say, that man was born just—from a just Father with respect to His divine nature and from a just mother with respect to His human nature—it is fitting to maintain that He had an original justice in the place of that original injustice which all other sons of Adam have at their origin.

CHAPTER XXI

WHY HE WAS UNABLE TO HAVE PERSONAL INJUSTICE

It is superfluous to argue that personal injustice did not touch Him, since there was never any human nature in Him without there also being a divine nature in Him, and since bodily corruption did not burden His soul against His will nor hinder His soul in any way. And this soul—indeed, this whole man and Word of God—is one person, who, being God, has always existed. Hence, according to His person as God, He always had perfect justice, wisdom, and power from Himself—even though according to His natures His human nature received all that it had from His divine nature.

I do not deny that there may be a better reason for explaining how God took from the sinful mass a man who had no sin, as if taking something unleavened from something leavened. And if there is a better argument than the one I have given here and in the *Cur Deus Homo,* then if it is shown to me I will gladly accept it. And I will not persist in my arguments if they can be shown to be false (though I doubt that they can be).

<h1 style="text-align:center">Chapter XXII</h1>

The Magnitude of Original Sin

Original sin can be neither something more nor something less than I have said, because as soon as an infant becomes rational, the human nature in that infant does not have the justice which it received in Adam and which it should always possess, nor does any inability ever excuse it for not having justice—as I have said above. Nevertheless, I do not think that original sin is as grave as I suggested earlier in this treatise. Because I wanted to show that original sin did not pertain to the man who was conceived from the Virgin, I stipulated that it was so grave that nothing more could be added to it; and, as I said, I did this so as not to seem to minimize its gravity with respect to the topic at hand. But I shall now speak briefly about my present opinion on that subject.

I do not think that the sin of Adam is passed down in infants in such a way that they ought to be punished for it, as if each of them had personally committed it himself just as Adam did. And I think this even though it has happened, on account of Adam's sin, that no one can be born without sin, which is followed by condemnation. For when the Apostle says that "death reigned from Adam unto Moses, even over those who had not sinned according to the likeness of Adam's transgression" (Rom. 5:14), he seems clearly to signify that neither the transgression of Adam nor anything else equally great is imputed to his descendants personally—even though the Apostle declares elsewhere in his writings that all the sons of Adam (with the exception of the Son of the Virgin) are "sinners" and "children of wrath" (Rom. 5:8; Eph. 2:3). For when he says, "even over those who had not sinned according to the likeness of Adam's transgression," we can understand this to mean "even over those who did not sin as much as Adam sinned when he transgressed." And when the Apostle says, "The law entered so that the offense might abound," he means one of two things: either (1) before the law entered, the sin in those "who did not sin according to the likeness of Adam's transgression" was less than Adam's sin or (2) after the law entered, sin abounded in men more than it did in Adam. But when I think about it, I do not see how the latter alternative could be true. For in the *Cur Deus Homo* you have already read my views concerning the weightiness of Adam's sin and its satisfaction. Nevertheless, unless there is a satisfaction for the sin through which human nature precipitated itself into evil, no one can be restored to that state for which man was created and for which a reproductive nature was given to him, and human nature cannot be rescued from those evils into which it fell.

Now, someone will ask, "If individuals do not have the sin of Adam, why do you maintain that no one is saved without there being satisfaction for Adam's sin? For how can a just God demand from them satisfaction for a sin which they do not have?" But, as I said in the *Cur Deus Homo,* God does not demand more than He ought to from any sinner; but since no sinner can repay as much as he owes, Christ alone made payment for those who are saved, repaying even more than they owe.

At this point we ought also to consider another reason why the sin in infants is less than the sin in Adam, even though sin is transmitted from him unto all men. For through one man, i.e., through Adam, "sin entered into the world, and through sin came death" (Rom. 5:12).

Chapter XXIII
Why and How Adam's Sin Was Transmitted to Infants

Unless we understand why and how the sin of Adam is present in infants, we shall not know why it is less in them than in Adam. Although we have previously said this in so far as it was necessary for the problem then at hand, nevertheless it will not be superfluous to repeat it briefly. Surely it cannot be denied that infants existed in Adam when he sinned. But they existed in Adam causally or materially as in a seed; and they exist in themselves personally. For in Adam they were the seed itself, while in themselves they are individual and different persons. In so far as they existed in Adam they were not different from Adam; but in so far as they exist in themselves they are different from him. In Adam they were Adam, but in themselves they are themselves. Therefore, all infants existed in Adam, but they did not exist in Adam themselves—since they themselves did not yet exist [i.e., exist personally].

Perhaps someone will say, "That existence in terms of which other men are said to have existed in Adam is so empty as to be nothing, and should not even be called existence." But then he should also say that the existence whereby Christ existed in Abraham and in David and in the other forefathers as their seed was also nothing or empty or false. And he should also term as "nothing" the existence whereby all those things that come from seeds were first in seeds; and he should also assert that God created nothing when He created the seminal existence of all those things which are later procreated from seeds. But such a seminal existence is not nothing; for if it were nothing, then those things which we see would not exist. For, unless those things which nature produces from seeds were first something in those seeds, then such things could not exist from these seeds in any way at all. But if these affirmations [viz., that the above-mentioned seminal existences are nothing] are simply foolish, then the existence by which all men were in Adam is not false or empty but is true and solid existence. So, too, God did not create an empty something when He created all men to exist in Adam in this way. But, as I said above, in him they were not different from him, and therefore they were far different from what they are in themselves.

Now, although it is true that all men were in Adam, nevertheless the Son of the Virgin alone was in Adam in a way vastly different from that of other men. For all others were in Adam in such a way that they existed from him through that reproductive nature which was subject to his power and his will, but Jesus alone was not in Adam in such a way that He existed from him through his reproductive nature or his will. Hence, at the time that Adam sinned it had been established that he was the one from whom all other men were going to exist—and going to exist by way of propagation. But, though it had been established that Adam was the one from whom Jesus was going to exist, yet Jesus was not going to exist from him by way of propagation—because it was not in Adam's power that Jesus should be propagated from him. And it was also not in Adam's power to make Jesus either from another being or from nothing. Hence, it did not lie within the power of Adam that Jesus should exist in any way. For it was neither in the power of his nature nor in the power of his will to cause Jesus to exist in any way whatsoever. Nevertheless, there did exist in Adam that nature from which Jesus was going to be propagated by the power of God (and not by the power of Adam). For even though the human will inseminated, and nature brought forth, offspring in the lineage from Adam to the Virgin Mother, so that the Virgin received her own existence from Adam in the same way that we all do (viz., partly by the natural order and partly by the voluntary order), nevertheless in the Virgin neither nature nor the will of the creature produced offspring; but rather "the Holy Spirit" and "the Power of the Most High" (Luke 1:35) miraculously begat a man from the Virgin Woman. Therefore, it was in Adam—that is, in his power of propagation—that all others [except Jesus] should exist from him. But it was not in Adam's power to cause Jesus to exist from him at all—just as it was not in the power of the clay from which the first man was created to cause Adam to exist from it by means of a miracle. Nor was it in Adam's power to cause Eve to exist from him in the miraculous way that she did. So, too, although Jesus existed in the lineage of persons from Adam to Mary, it was not in the power of any of these persons to cause Him to exist. Nevertheless, Jesus existed in them; for just as the first man existed in the clay from which he was created, and just as Eve existed in Adam from whom she was created—though neither of them was created by the will or power of the creature, but solely by the power of God—so, too, Jesus existed in those from whom He was to be assumed, He existed in His ancestors. And to the extent that being made God-man is greater than being made mere man, to that same extent is the grace and miracle of Jesus' begottenness greater than that of Adam's and Eve's. Hence, at the time Adam sinned, Jesus was in Adam in a quite different way from those who are begotten from Adam through the natural and voluntary course. There is, then, a certain sense in which Adam does make other men whenever the human will and human nature procreate them through a power which the will and nature have received from God. But God alone made Jesus, although He made Him from Adam. For He did not make Jesus through Adam, but through Himself and, as it were, from Himself.

Therefore, what is more suitable for showing the magnitude of God's goodness and the plenitude of grace granted to Adam than that Adam, who had the power to cause other men who existed through him to be what he was by nature, also be given the freedom of choice by which to propagate men who would have the same quality of justice and happiness that he had? And this *was* given him. But, even though Adam was established in such lofty grace, he nonetheless freely deserted the goods which were given him and which were to be kept for himself and for his posterity. For this reason his descendants lost that which their father could have given them by keeping, but which he took away from them by not keeping. To understand this fully we must carefully consider pure justice, giving no heed to our prejudices (which often hinder the mind from understanding what is right). And if we do this, then it seems to me that what I have said above constitutes a sufficient reason for the sin and evils of Adam to descend to infants. Nonetheless, I shall say a bit more about my views concerning the way that Adam's sin is transmitted to his descendants.

Earlier I said that there is a sin which comes from a person and a sin which comes from a nature. The sin which comes from a person can be called personal sin, and the sin which comes from a nature can be called natural, or original, sin. Now, just as what is personal passes over into what is natural, so what is natural passes over into what is personal. For example, nature required that Adam eat something, because it was nature's ordained role to make such a requirement. But when Adam ate the fruit of the forbidden tree, it was not a natural will, but his own personal will that did this. Nevertheless, although the person did this thing, he did not do it apart from his nature. For the first man was a person in so far as he was called Adam; and he was a nature in so far as he was called man. The person, therefore, made the nature sinful, because when Adam sinned man sinned. Indeed, it was not because he was man that he was impelled to partake of what was forbidden; rather, he was drawn to this by his own desire and will—which originated in his person and not in his nature. But this order of nature and person is reversed in the infants who are conceived from Adam. For the fact that the justice which they should have is not in them is not the fault of a personal will (as it was in Adam's case) but results because the nature which they received from Adam lacks this justice. For in Adam human nature—which did not exist outside of him at the time he sinned—was stripped of the justice which it possessed; and it forever after lacks justice unless it is aided by God. Hence, because human nature subsists in persons and because persons do not exist without natures, human nature causes the persons of infants to be sinful. So in Adam the person deprived human nature of the good of justice; and human nature, thus impoverished, causes all those persons whom it procreates from itself to be sinful and unjust because of the same need of justice. In this way the personal sin of Adam passes unto all those who are propagated from him, even though in them it is not personal sin but natural (or original) sin.

So it is clear that there is a great difference between the magnitude of Adam's sin and that of those who are propagated from him. Because Adam sinned by his own will, his progeny sin by that necessity of nature which the personal will of Adam merited for its sin. But, although no one thinks that unequal sins are followed by equal penalties, nevertheless the condemnation for personal and original sin is similar, inasmuch as no one who has sinned in either way will be admitted into the Kingdom of God (for which end man was made) except by means of the death of Christ, which alone remits the debt incurred by the sin of Adam. For, even though not all men deserve equal torment in Hell [yet they all do deserve, apart from the death of Christ, to be excluded from the Kingdom of God]. For after the day of judgment every angel and every man will be either in the Kingdom of God or in Hell. So we see that the sin of infants is less than the sin of Adam, and that nevertheless no one is saved in any way other than by means of that universal satisfaction through which every sin—both great and small—is remitted. And so far as God has enabled me I have already discussed in the *Cur Deus Homo* why there is no salvation without the death of Christ and how salvation comes to man through Christ's death.

CHAPTER XXIV

THAT THE SINS OF OUR ANCESTORS WHO LIVED AFTER ADAM ARE NOT RECKONED IN THE ORIGINAL SIN OF THEIR DESCENDANTS

I do not think that the sins of our recent ancestors are a part of original sin. Indeed, had Adam not been able to transmit his own justice to those who were going to be generated from him, then he would also not have been able to transmit his own injustice to them. By the same kind of reasoning, since no one who lives after Adam is able to keep justice for his own offspring [for such a person has received from Adam no justice to transmit], I see no reason why the sins of recent ancestors should be imputed to the souls of their children. For there is no doubt that infants do not keep uprightness of will for its own sake; and so they are all equally unjust because they do not have that justice which every human being ought to have. This utter lack of justice is transmitted to all human beings from Adam, in whom human nature deprived itself of this same justice. For, although human nature in Adam retained some justice—so that it could keep an upright will in some things—nevertheless, human nature was deprived of that gift by which it could have kept justice for itself in Adam's posterity. As a result, human nature was not able to propagate itself with any justice in any of Adam's offspring. Surely, all that human nature could remove from itself in infants was justice, together with the happiness which is given only to those who possess the required justice.

Thus, it does not seem possible that the injustice of our recent ancestors could increase the deprivation of justice in human nature. This deprivation is already such that no greater deprivation can descend to infants from the sin of Adam. For where there is already no justice, no justice can be taken away. And where no justice can be removed, no injustice can be added. Therefore, unjust ancestors are able to add no other injustice to their children than this deprivation of justice which we are discussing [viz., that which comes from Adam]. But some justice can always be given where none exists. So, if unjust ancestors are said to add any injustice to their children, then it seems both more possible and probable that just ancestors can give justice to their descendants. But if this happens, the infant descendants of just ancestors have some kind of justice; and then these infants—if they die without baptism—would be condemned less severely than the children of unjust ancestors. Or, if the children of just ancestors were saved, then they would be saved by virtue of having some antecedent merit. But the

Apostle Paul denies such a thing when, by referring to Jacob and Esau, he proves that no infant is saved except by a grace which is antecedent to the merits of all infants alike. Therefore, since just ancestors do not give justice to their own descendants prior to their descendants' baptism, unjust ancestors do not add injustice to their descendants.

But someone may say:

"It is true that unjust ancestors do not add any injustice to their descendants, inasmuch as they are unable to remove any justice from them. But they do cause that original injustice which their descendants have from Adam to affect them more seriously. Conversely, just ancestors cause the original injustice which their descendants have from Adam to affect them less seriously. For this reason, if children of just ancestors are less unjust than children of unjust ancestors, then they ought not to be condemned as much as the children of unjust ancestors."

But let that person dare to say this only if he can prove it. I, for one, do not dare to say this when I see that the children both of the just and of the unjust are variously elected to, or reprobated from, the grace of baptism. But, even if anyone dares to propose the above argument, he cannot prove it. For certainly a man only becomes more just the more willing he is to seek or to avoid what he ought; in the same way a man only becomes more unjust the more he loves or despises what he ought not. But if it cannot be shown that as soon as infants have a soul, some will more and others will less what they ought or ought not, then no one can prove that some children are begotten more or less just than others. Therefore, as the justice of just ancestors is seen not to mitigate the original injustice of their children, so the injustice of unjust ancestors is seen not to aggravate the original injustice of theirs. So, if unjust ancestors are unable to increase the original sin of their children (either in number of sins or in their magnitude), then it seems to me that the sins of their ancestors since Adam are not included in the original sin of infants.

I do not deny that many goods and great benefits abound to
the souls and to the bodies of offspring on account of the merits
of their ancestors. Nor do I deny that children and grandchil-
dren "unto the third and fourth generation"[8] (and perhaps
even longer) are scourged with various tribulations in this life
on account of the sins of their ancestors. And, although it would
take too long to introduce examples, I do not even deny that
children lose goods of the soul which might have accrued to them
had their parents been just. But I do maintain that original sin
is present to the same extent in all infants who are conceived
naturally—just as the sin of Adam, which is the cause of
infants' being conceived in sin, pertains to all men equally.

Chapter XXV

How the Sins of Ancestors Harm the Souls of Their Descendants

But if the sins of ancestors ever harm the souls of their
descendants, then I think it occurs in this manner: God does
not impute the sins of their ancestors to them, nor does He
lead them into any transgression on account of their ancestors;
but God does sometimes abandon men to their own sins on
account of the sins of their unjust ancestors (just as He often
rescues men from sin on account of the merits of their just
ancestors). For, since no one is free from sin unless God sets him
free, then when God does not set someone free from sin, we say
that God leads him into sin; and when God does not soften a
man's heart, we say that God hardens his heart. So, if it is said
that God punishes the sinful soul on account of the sins of unjust
ancestors, then it seems more credible to think that God does this
by abandoning the sinful soul (to which He owes nothing but
punishment) to its own sins than to think that God does this by
burdening the sinful soul with the sins of other men—torment-
ing it because of other men's sins rather than because of its own.

8. Ex. 20:5.

So, therefore, without contradicting the fact that God visits the sins of parents upon their children (and even upon their children's souls) "unto the third and fourth generation," and without contradicting anything else we read in Scripture which seems to signify that the sins of parents harm the souls of their children, we can affirm that original sin is of the same magnitude in all men, and also that "the son will not bear the iniquity of his father" (Ez. 18:20), and that "each one shall bear his own burden" (Gal. 6:5), and that "everyone will receive good or evil in accordance with what he has done in the body" (II Cor. 5:10). For, indeed, the soul of the son does not die on account of the sin of his father, but only because of its own; nor when the child is left in his own iniquity does he bear his father's iniquity, but only his own. And the child does not bear another's burden, but only his own; and the son does not receive good and evil in accordance with his father's deeds, but only in accordance with what he has done in the body. However, on account of the sins of his unjust ancestors the son has not been freed from his own evil deeds; and in this manner the iniquities which he bears are imputed [by Scripture] to the sins of his ancestors.

CHAPTER XXVI
HOW, NEVERTHELESS,
NO ONE BEARS THE SIN OF HIS ANCESTORS,
BUT ONLY HIS OWN SIN

But perhaps someone may object that because all those who are not saved by faith in Christ bear the burden of Adam's iniquity, it follows that either (a) infants also ought to bear the iniquity of their other ancestors as well or else (b) they ought not bear the iniquity of Adam. Now let anyone who makes this objection carefully consider the fact that infants do not bear Adam's iniquity, but bear their own. For Adam's sin is something different from the sin of infants—inasmuch as Adam's sin is a cause, and infants' sin an effect. Adam was deprived of required justice because he himself, and not another, deserted it; but infants are deprived of justice because someone else, and not themselves, deserted it. Therefore, the sin of Adam and the sin of infants are not the same thing. And when the Apostle says (as I mentioned earlier) that "death reigned from Adam unto Moses, even over those who had not sinned according to the likeness of Adam's transgression" (Rom. 5:14), then just as he indicates that the sin of infants is less than the sin of Adam, so also he clearly shows that their sin is something different from Adam's.

So, then, when an infant is condemned on account of original sin, he is not condemned for Adam's sin but for his own; for if he did not have sin of his own, he would not be condemned. Hence, an infant bears his own iniquity and not Adam's, even though Scripture says that he bears the iniquity of Adam because Adam's sin was the cause of his own sin. But the power which Adam had to cause his descendants to be born in sin does not belong to any of our other ancestors, because human nature in these ancestors has no power to beget offspring who are just [and unless it is possible for human nature to bestow justice upon its offspring, it is not possible for it to remove justice from them]. Therefore, although there is sin in infants as a result of Adam's sin, there is no additional sin in them as a result of the iniquities of their other ancestors.

CHAPTER XXVII
WHAT ORIGINAL SIN IS,
AND THAT IT IS OF EQUAL MAGNITUDE
IN ALL HUMAN BEINGS

Therefore, I think that original sin is only that sin which is in an infant at the moment he has a rational soul. And I think this regardless of any corruption that was in his body, or its members, before it received a soul, and regardless of anything that might happen to either his body or his soul after the moment in which the body receives a soul. And I have presented arguments to explain why original sin is of equal magnitude in all infants who are propagated in accordance with the natural order and why all who die in this sin alone are equally condemned. Whatever sin accrues to a man above and beyond original sin is personal sin; for as a human person is born sinful because of his nature, so his nature can be made more sinful because of the person—for when any human person sins he sins as a man.

I am unable to understand original sin in infants as anything other than the lack of required justice which occurred through the disobedience of Adam. Through this lack of required justice we are all children of wrath, since the voluntary desertion of justice accuses the human nature which acted in Adam, and the inability to recover justice in no way excuses the persons who are made having Adam's nature. The utter lack of happiness also accompanies the desertion of justice, so that all human persons are born lacking not only all justice but also all happiness. In the exile of this life these two deprivations leave all men defenseless and exposed to sins and miseries which constantly befall them, attacking them on every side (except in so far as they are protected by divine providence).

CHAPTER XXVIII
AGAINST THOSE WHO DO NOT THINK
THAT INFANTS SHOULD BE CONDEMNED

There are those who do not wish to accept the view that infants who die without having been baptized should be condemned solely on the basis of the injustice which I have been discussing. Their reasoning is that no man judges infants to be blameworthy for the sin of another person, and infants are not just and rational as long as they remain infants, nor should God judge these innocent babes more severely than men judge them.

But it must be replied to men of this opinion that God should act differently with respect to infants from the way man should act. For man should not demand from human nature what he himself has not given to human nature and what is not owed to him by human nature. A man does not justly blame someone else for being born with guilt when he himself cannot be born without the same guilt and when he can only be cleansed from this guilt by another. But God rightly demands from human nature what He has given to it and what human nature justly owes to Him.

But, if we think about it, God's judgment in condemning infants is not much different from the judgment of men. For suppose that some man and his wife, who have been elevated to great dignity and wealth by pure favor and not by their own merit, were both to commit a serious and unpardonable crime, so that they were justly cast down from their position and given into servitude. In this case, who shall say that the children born to them after their condemnation should not also be subjected to servitude, but ought rather to be gratuitously restored to the goods which their parents justly lost? But this is the situation of our first parents, who through their own fault were justly condemned from happiness into wretchedness, and so begat their children into the same exile. Now, although we ought to judge like cases by like standards, to the degree that the transgression of our first parents can be shown to be more blamable than that of the man and wife mentioned above, to that same degree ought our first parents to be judged more severely.

Finally, every man is either saved or condemned. Every man who is saved is admitted into the Kingdom of Heaven, and every man who is condemned is excluded from it. He who is admitted is elevated to the likeness of those angels in whom there never was or will be any sin; but this elevation cannot occur as long as there is any taint of sin in him. So it is impossible for a man to be saved if he has any sin, however small. Therefore, if what I have called "original sin" is any sin at all, then it is necessary for every man who is born in original sin to be condemned for it—unless it has been removed from him.

CHAPTER XXIX
HOW THE INABILITY TO HAVE JUSTICE EXCUSES INFANTS AFTER BAPTISM

I have said that the inability to have justice does not excuse the injustice of infants. But perhaps someone will ask:

"If there is sin (i.e., injustice) in infants before they are baptized, and if you say that the inability to have justice is inexcusable, and if Christian baptism removes only the sin that precedes baptism, then since an infant is without justice for as long as he is an infant in the period following his baptism (for if justice is uprightness of will kept for its own sake, an infant cannot even understand the justice which he should keep), why isn't an infant unjust even after he is baptized? If a baptized person dies in infancy before he knows how to repent (though not dying immediately after baptism), then since he does not have the required justice and since his inability to have it is no excuse, he is in an unjust state when he dies (as if he had died before baptism) and so is not admitted into the Kingdom of God—since no unjust person enters therein. But the Catholic Church does not believe that baptized infants who die before they know how to repent are excluded from the Kingdom of God. On the other hand, if baptism removes the future sin of infancy, then why doesn't it also remove those future sins which a person will commit later in his life?"

I reply that baptism completely blots out all the sins which existed before baptism. For this reason the original inability to have justice which was imputed as sin to infants before they were baptized is not imputed to them afterwards. The inability to have justice could not excuse the absence of justice before baptism, since this inability is culpable; but even though this inability remains after baptism, it excuses the absence of justice because it is no longer culpable. Whence it follows that justice, which infants owed before they were baptized and for which they could offer no excuse, is not required of them as a kind of obligation after they are baptized. For as long as their only reason for not having justice is their original [i.e., natural] inability to have it, they are not unjust, since there is no lack of *required* justice in them. For one has no obligation concerning that which, through no fault of his own, is impossible. Therefore, if baptized infants die before they know how to repent, they are not unjust; rather they are saved as if they were just—saved both by means of the justice of Christ, who gave Himself for them, and by means of the justice of faith on the part of the Church, their Mother, who believes on their behalf.

More out of conjecture than out of certainty I have discussed original sin to the best of my understanding, and I shall hold my present views until God makes known to me some better understanding. But if someone else has a different interpretation, I shall not reject his opinion—or anyone else's—provided it can be proved to be true.

On the Procession of the Holy Spirit
(De Processione Spiritus Sancti)

Chapter I

The Greeks deny a doctrine which we Latins confess, namely, that the Holy Spirit proceeds from the Son. They also reject our Latin doctors whom we follow in this teaching. Now, the Greeks revere the Gospels with us Latins, and they also believe in common with us all the other doctrines about the trine and one God. Therefore, if they choose to acquiesce in sound truth rather than to contend for an empty victory, I hope that through the help of this same Spirit they can be led rationally from that which they confess without hesitation to that which they do not yet accept. There are many who are capable of accomplishing this task better than I. Nevertheless, since this task is imposed upon me by many whose petitions I dare not resist—because of their affection and their religious desire, as well as because of our duty to love the truth—I invoke the same Holy Spirit that He might condescend to lead me to accomplish this. In this hope I shall undertake what many request. By using the faith of the Greeks, along with those things which they believe and confess without any doubt, I shall demonstrate by means of most certain arguments what they do not believe. On account of the lowliness of my knowledge I shall leave higher matters to more learned men.

The Greeks believe that God is one, unique, and perfect. They do not believe that He has any parts, but rather that He is wholly whatever He is. They also confess God to be Father, Son, and Holy Spirit. Therefore, whether God be spoken of singly (as Father, or Son, or Holy Spirit), or two at the same time (Father and Son, or Father and Holy Spirit, or Son and Holy Spirit), or three at the same time (Father, Son, and Holy Spirit), the same whole and perfect God is designated—although the name ''Father'' or the name ''Son'' does not signify the same thing as the name ''God.'' For it is not the same thing to be God as it is to be Father or Son; and the name ''Holy Spirit'' is used as a relative name because ''Holy Spirit'' is understood as the spirit of someone. For, although the Father is a spirit and holy and the Son is a spirit and holy, nevertheless neither the Father nor the Son is the spirit of someone as the Holy Spirit is the spirit of someone. For the Holy Spirit is the Spirit of God and also the Spirit of the Father and of the Son. And even though the Greeks deny that the Spirit proceeds from the Son, they do not deny Him to be the Spirit of the Son.

The Greeks also believe and confess that God exists from God by being begotten and that God exists from God by proceeding. This is so because God the Son exists from God the Father by being begotten and God the Holy Spirit exists from God the Father by proceeding. And they do not think that God who is begotten is another God than the one from whom He is begotten, nor do they think that God who proceeds is another God than the one from whom He proceeds. But, according to the signifying names, the fact that there is one from whom someone is begotten, and that there is one who is begotten from another, and that there is one who proceeds from another, allows a plurality. In accordance with this fact, Father, Son, and Holy Spirit are plural and different from one another. For when God is said to be Father, He is signified to be the one from whom another is begotten. And when He is called Son, He is understood to be the one who is begotten from another. And when He is called Holy

Spirit, He is shown to be the one who proceeds from another—because He is not understood simply (*absolute*) as a spirit, but as Spirit of God. For when it is said that the Son is from the Father, or that the Holy Spirit is from the Father, it is understood that whatever the Son is or whatever the Holy Spirit is, He is from the Father. But the Son is understood to be from the Father in one way and the Holy Spirit in another. For the Son is from His Father, that is, from God who is His Father; while the Holy Spirit is not from God *His* Father, but only from God who is Father. Therefore, the Son, with respect to His being from God, is called the Father's Son; and the one from whom the Son exists is called His Father. But the Holy Spirit, with respect to His being from God, is not the Father's Son; nor does He exist from one who is His Father.

Now, it is certain that God is not the Father of anyone, or the Son of anyone, or the Spirit of anyone except of God; nor is God anything except the same Father, Son, and Holy Spirit. And just as there is one God, so there is only one Father, one Son, and one Holy Spirit. Hence, it happens that in the Trinity there is no Father except of the Son, nor any Son except of the Father, nor a Holy Spirit as the spirit of anyone other than of the Father and the Son. This therefore is the only cause of plurality in God, namely, that the names "Father," "Son," and "Holy Spirit" cannot all be predicated of one another. For the persons are distinct from one another because God is from God in the two ways mentioned above.

All of what we have said above can be expressed by the noun "relation." For, since the Son exists from God by being begotten and the Holy Spirit exists from God by proceeding, then by this very diversity of birth and procession they are related to each other as diverse and distinct from each other. When one substance exists from another substance, two incompatible relations come into being if the substances are referred to according to these relations. For when a man exists by being begotten from another man, then the one from whom the man exists is called father, and the man who exists from the other man is called son. Therefore, it is impossible for a father to be his own son or for a son to be his own father. But nothing prohibits a father from being a son or a son from being a father, when one man is both father and son because he is father to one and son to another. For example, when Isaac is the father of Jacob and the son of Abraham, a father is a son and a son is a father without contradiction. For Isaac is called father in relation to someone other than his own father, and he is called son in relation to someone other than his own son. Moreover, it is impossible that Isaac the father be his own son; and it is impossible that Isaac the son be his own father.

The same thing applies to God. For God is Father, Son, and Holy Spirit; and there is no Father except of the Son, no Son except of the Father, and no Spirit of anyone except of the Father and the Son. Hence, the Father is not the Son or the Holy Spirit; the Son is not the Father; nor is the Holy Spirit the Father. Indeed, both the Son and the Holy Spirit are from the Father; and the one from whom another exists cannot be that other who exists from him, nor can that one who exists from another be the one from whom he exists (as has been explained). For this reason, the Father is not the Son or the Holy Spirit; nor is the Son or the Holy Spirit the Father. Moreover, the Holy Spirit is not the Son, and the Son is not the Holy Spirit—though I must explain this with a different reason for the moment, since it is not yet established that the Holy Spirit exists and proceeds from the Son. So for the moment, we may say that the Son is different from the Holy Spirit because the Son exists by being begotten from the Father, whereas the Holy Spirit exists by proceeding. Also, the Son cannot be His own spirit, nor can the Holy Spirit be the one whose spirit He is.

Having finished these preliminary remarks, let us inquire how the indivisible unity and the incompatible plurality in God are related to each other. The Greeks and we Latins equally believe and indubitably confess these things which have been said above. Although we Latins say that the Holy Spirit proceeds from the Son, and although the Greeks do not sympathize with us concerning this matter, yet we all ought unequivocally to affirm by common consent those things which follow necessarily from these mutually shared premises. From the property of the unity of

God (a unity which has no parts) it follows that anything which is said about the one God, who is wholly whatever He is, is said about the whole of God the Father, and about the whole of God the Son, and about the whole of God the Holy Spirit. This is so because each one alone is wholly and perfectly God. But the aforementioned opposition of relation, which originates from those two ways in which God is from God, prohibits our calling any one of the persons by the names of the other two; and it also prohibits our attributing to any of the three persons properties peculiar to one of them alone. Therefore, the consequences which follow from this unity [of substance] and from this relation [of persons] are ordered so that the plurality which follows from the relation does not apply to those things which have the simplicity of the unity we have discussed, and so that the unity does not limit the plurality whenever this same relation is signified. Thus, on the one hand, the unity does not lose that which follows from it, except when some opposition of relation stands against it; and, on the other hand, the relation does not lose what belongs to it [viz., plurality], except when the inseparable unity opposes it.

This conclusion will become clearer if we consider some examples. It is easy to understand how the simplicity of unity excludes from itself the plurality which is contained in the signification of the relational names. For we confess that the Father is not the Son or the Holy Spirit; nor is the Son the Father or the Holy Spirit; nor is the Holy Spirit the Father or the Son. Therefore, it follows that Father, Son, and Holy Spirit are distinct from one another and are plural. But the Father is God, the Son is God, and the Holy Spirit is God. Hence, what could follow with greater force (if this plurality of persons retains its property) than the conclusion that Father, Son, and Holy Spirit are several gods and distinct from one another? But the inviolable simplicity of deity, by which we believe that there is only one God, does not allow this conclusion. So the unity of God's essence opposes our drawing this consequence from the relational names.

We must also, by first taking one of the cases where no opposition of relation interferes, consider how the plurality of persons will prevent us from drawing the consequence of unity. We say that the one God is Father, Son, and Holy Spirit, and that whether we speak of one, or of two, or of three at the same time, they are one and the same God. Therefore, if God is eternal, it necessarily follows from the unity of deity that the Father is eternal, the Son is eternal, and the Holy Spirit is eternal. And since they are one God, whether taken singularly or plurally, there is only one eternal God. The same consequence follows if God is called Creator or just or any other such thing which does not signify a relation.[1] Now let us see how the notion of relation restricts our drawing this consequence of the unity of God. For we say that God is the Father; and since Father, Son, and Holy Spirit are one God, the unity of God demands that the Son be the Father and that the Holy Spirit be the Father. But the relation, which prohibits the Son or the Holy Spirit from being the Father, opposes such a consequence. For nature does not permit, nor does understanding grasp, either of the two following situations: (1) that a being existing from someone else is identical with the one from whom he exists; or (2) that the one from whom he exists is identical with this being who exists from him. But the Son and the Holy Spirit exist from the Father. Therefore, neither the Son nor the Holy Spirit can be the Father, even though God be Father, and even though one and the same God be Father, Son, and Holy Spirit. The same thing holds if it is said that God is the Son. For the consequence of the unity of God demands that both Father and Holy Spirit be the Son. But the Father from whom the Son exists cannot be the Son who exists from Him; and the Holy Spirit, who exists from the Father by proceeding, cannot be the one who exists from the Father by being begotten. It is the same when it is said that God is the Holy Spirit. The unity of God demands that both Father and Son be the Holy Spirit. But the Father from whom the Holy Spirit exists cannot be the Holy Spirit who exists from Him; and the Son, who exists from the Father by being begotten, cannot be the one who exists from the same Father by proceeding—viz., the

1. On the distinction between referring to God relatively and referring to Him substantially, note Augustine, *De Trinitate*, Bk. 5 (PL, 42:916 ff.).

Holy Spirit. And after we show that the Holy Spirit exists from the Son, then it will also be clear that because of this relation the Son cannot be the Holy Spirit and that the Holy Spirit cannot be the Son.

Let us consider here how the above-mentioned oppositions of relation limit the consequences of the unity described above. God exists from God. Therefore, once this has been accepted—and since the same God is Father, Son, and Holy Spirit—it follows according to this identity that God the Father is God from God and also God from whom God exists. And, similarly, the Son is God from God and also God from whom God exists. And the same thing may be said about the Holy Spirit. But to ask if each one is God from whom God exists is no different from considering whether each one is God from God. For God cannot be from God except as Father, or Son, or Holy Spirit. And God cannot be from God unless He is from the Father, or from the Son, or from the Holy Spirit. Therefore, let us consider whether each one is God from God, and it will become clear whether or not each one is God from whom God exists.[2]

Now, according to that opposition of relation we have discussed above, the Father cannot be from God. For God does not exist except as Father, or Son, or Holy Spirit, or as two or three of these at the same time. And so God the Father cannot exist from God unless He exists from the Father (that is, from Himself), or from the Son, or from the Holy Spirit, or from two or three of these at the same time. But He cannot exist from Himself, since the one existing from someone and the someone from whom he exists cannot be the same. Nor does God the Father exist from the Son, since the Son exists from Him; and

2. Anselm's argument throughout this treatise distinguishes two notions: (A) God from whom God exists and (B) God from God. God the Father is A because the Son is begotten from Him and because the Holy Spirit proceeds from Him; He is not B, since He neither proceeds nor is begotten. God the Son is B since He is begotten; and He is A since the Holy Spirit proceeds also from Him. God the Holy Spirit is B since He proceeds from the Father and the Son; but He is not A, since neither the Father nor the Son proceeds from Him or is begotten from Him. In Chap. 15 Anselm summarizes these distinctions.

so He cannot exist from the Son. Nor does He exist from the
Holy Spirit, since the Holy Spirit exists from Him; and so the
Father cannot be the one who exists from Him. And by reason of
the same opposition of relation He cannot exist from two or three
persons at the same time. But it is necessary that God the Son
exist from God the Father, because the Father does not exist
from the Son. And the Son cannot exist from the Son, i.e., from
Himself, because the one existing from someone and the someone
from whom he exists are not the same. However, whether the
Son exists from the Holy Spirit or whether the Holy Spirit exists
from the Son will be shown later. But we shall first inquire, in
the light of our previous conclusions, whether or not the Holy
Spirit exists from the Father and also from Himself. Now, it is
necessary that the Holy Spirit exist from the Father, because no
opposition of relation opposes this; for the Father does not exist
from the Holy Spirit. And it is impossible that the Holy Spirit
exist from Himself, since the one existing from someone and the
someone from whom he exists cannot be the same. In all these
things nothing except one of the aforementioned oppositions
opposes the consequence of God's unique identity. And what we
have understood in these cases must also be understood always to
apply to every other case of speaking about God.

Now, on the basis of the above irrefutable arguments, it must
be asked whether the Son exists from the Holy Spirit or whether
the Holy Spirit exists from the Son. I have shown that either the
Father exists from the Son or the Son exists from the Father,
and that either the Father exists from the Holy Spirit or the
Holy Spirit exists from the Father. Now, for the same reason, I
affirm that either the Son exists from the Holy Spirit or the Holy
Spirit exists from the Son. Whoever denies this must also deny
that God is only one (*unum solum*), or that the Son is God, or
that the Holy Spirit is God, or that God exists from God—for
my affirmation follows from these premises. Furthermore,
neither the Son nor the Holy Spirit exists from the Father in any
other way than from the Father's essence, which is common to
Him with the Son and the Holy Spirit. Therefore, when it is said

that the Son exists from God the Father, then if Father and Holy Spirit are one and the same God, it follows according to the unity of deity that the Son exists from the Holy Spirit. In the same way, when we confess that the Holy Spirit exists from God the Father, then if Father and Son are one and the same God, it follows according to the same unity of deity that the Holy Spirit exists from the Son. Therefore, it is clearly known from these arguments that either the Son exists from the Holy Spirit or the Holy Spirit exists from the Son. For one of these assertions must be true and the other false.

Now if it can be demonstrated that the Son does not exist from the Holy Spirit, then it must follow that the Holy Spirit exists from the Son. But someone might argue that ''Even though the Holy Spirit does not exist from the Son, it does not follow that the Son exists from the Father and from the Holy Spirit simply because Father and Holy Spirit are one God. Or even though the Son does not exist from the Holy Spirit, it does not follow that the Holy Spirit exists from the Father and from the Son simply because Father and Son are one God.'' If anyone argues like this, let him consider that God is from God in one of the following ways: (1) as the whole is from the whole; (2) as a part is from a part; (3) as the whole is from a part; or (4) as a part is from the whole. But God has no parts. Therefore, it is impossible that God exist from God as the whole from a part, or as a part from the whole, or as a part from a part. So it follows that if God exists from God, the whole exists from the whole. Therefore, if the Son is said to exist from God, who is Father and Holy Spirit, then two alternatives arise: either (1) the Father is one whole and the Holy Spirit another whole, so that the Son exists from the whole of the Father and not from the whole of the Holy Spirit; or (2) the Father and the Holy Spirit are the same whole God, so that the Son exists from that one whole which is both Father and Holy Spirit, and hence is equally from the Father and from the Holy Spirit—provided there is no reason to reject this conclusion. In the same way, if it is said that the Holy Spirit exists from the whole God, who is Father and Son, then two alternatives arise: either (1) the Father is one whole and the Son another, so that the Holy Spirit exists from the whole Father and not from the whole Son; or (2) the Father and the Son are the same whole, so that if the Holy Spirit exists from the Father, He must also exist from the Son—unless the Son exists from Him. For no other reason can be given for denying that the Holy Spirit exists from the Son.

Now someone will argue:

"Suppose that since the Father and the Holy Spirit are one God, and since the Son exists from the Father, it follows that the Son also exists from the Holy Spirit; or suppose that since the Father and the Son are one and the same God, and since the Holy Spirit exists from the Father, it follows that the Holy Spirit also exists from the Son. If the Father begets the Son, the Father must also beget the Holy Spirit—since the Son and the Holy Spirit are one and the same God. And if the Holy Spirit proceeds from the Father, then because the Son and the Holy Spirit have the same unity of deity, the Son also proceeds from the Father in the same way as the Holy Spirit. But if the unity of God in the Son and Holy Spirit does not lead us to conclude that each is begotten by or proceeds from the Father in the same way, then it seems that from the fact of the Father and the Holy Spirit's being one God it does not follow that the Son exists from the Holy Spirit, or that from the fact of the Father and the Son's being one God it does not follow that the Holy Spirit exists from the Son—as you have argued above."

I reply to this argument as follows: Both the Son and the Holy Spirit exist from the Father, but in different ways—one by being begotten and the other by proceeding. And this is why they are different from each other, as I have said. Hence, if one is begotten, the one who is distinct from him because he is not similarly begotten, but proceeds, cannot be begotten along with him. And if one proceeds, the one who is distinct from him because he does not similarly proceed, but is begotten, cannot proceed together with him. Therefore the unity of God does not lead to the conclusion suggested above, because the conclusion does not take account of the plurality which arises from the notions of begetting and proceeding. For even if the Son and the Holy Spirit were not plural for any other reason, then they would be different by virtue of this one thing. So when I assert that "either the Son exists from the Holy Spirit or the Holy Spirit exists from the Son" (because the Father is one God with the Son or with the Holy Spirit), I signify no plurality which could contradict the consequence drawn from unity. For I do not affirm that "*both* the Son exists from the Holy Spirit *and* the Holy Spirit exists from the Son," but rather that "*either* the Son exists from the Holy Spirit *or* the Holy Spirit exists from the Son."

We must therefore conclude with absolute and irrefutable necessity that if the above-mentioned things are true (things which we believe the same as do the Greeks), then either the Son exists from the Holy Spirit or the Holy Spirit exists from the Son. But that the Son does not exist from the Holy Spirit is known clearly from the Catholic faith.[3] For God only exists from God either by being begotten (as is the Son) or by proceeding (as does the Holy Spirit). But the Son is not begotten from the Holy Spirit. For, if the Son were begotten from the Holy Spirit, He would be the son of the Holy Spirit, and the Holy Spirit would be His father. But neither the Holy Spirit nor the Son is the father or the son of the other. Therefore, the Son is not begotten from the Holy Spirit.

And it is no less clear that the Son does not proceed from the Holy Spirit, for then the Son would be the spirit of the same Holy Spirit. But this is obviously false, since the Holy Spirit is believed to be, and is called, the Spirit of the Son; and the Son cannot be the spirit of His own spirit. Hence, the Son does not proceed from the Holy Spirit. Therefore, the Son is in no way from the Holy Spirit. And so it follows by an irrefutable argument that the Holy Spirit exists from the Son just as He also exists from the Father.

3. "*Fides catholica*" in this context refers primarily to the Quicumque.

Chapter II

Perhaps the Greeks will deny that the Holy Spirit is God from God in the same way that the Son is God from God, now that we can prove from this that the Holy Spirit exists and proceeds from the Son. For this doctrine is also not set forth in the creed[4] to which we Latins have added that the Holy Spirit exists and proceeds from the Son, and for which addition the Greeks censure us. But if the Greeks deny that the Holy Spirit is God from God, then they thereby deny either that the Father from whom the Holy Spirit exists is God, or that the Holy Spirit who exists from the Father is God, or that the essence of the Holy Spirit is derived from the Father. But no Christian denies that either the Father or the Holy Spirit is God. Let us therefore see whether the Holy Spirit in that which He is essentially is from (of) the Father. I have noticed that a certain bishop in the city of Bari, who is perhaps favorable toward the Greeks, is unwilling to support this view. Now, given that the Holy Spirit and the Father are one and the same God, then if the Holy Spirit does not exist from the Father, He cannot be found to be a different person from the Father. The reason that the Holy Spirit is a different person from the Father is not that the one does not have a son while the other does. Because one has a son while another does not *shows* that they are different persons; however, having or not having a son is not the *reason* they are different persons. Consider the example of two men, one of whom has a son while the other does not. Although from this fact they can be shown to be different persons, nevertheless it is not because of this fact that they are different persons—for whether either has a son or does not have a son, each one exists and is different from the other. Thus, the reason that the Father and the Holy Spirit are different from each other is not that one has a son and the other does not. But because they are different, nothing prohibits

4. The Nicene-Constantinople Creed (381) is under discussion throughout this treatise.

the one from having a son and the other from not having a
son.

Now, if it is said that the Son is a different person because the
Holy Spirit does not proceed from Him as the Spirit proceeds
from the Father, then we can reply in the same way. (For the
moment let me speak as if I were in agreement with the Greeks,
who deny that the Holy Spirit proceeds from the Son.) The Son
is not a different person from the Father simply because He does
not have the Holy Spirit proceeding from Him, as the Father
does. (For if this were the reason for the difference, it would
follow that if the Holy Spirit *did* proceed from the Son, Father
and Son would not be different persons.) Likewise, the Holy
Spirit is not a different person from the Father simply because
He does not have a son or a spirit proceeding from Himself—as
does the Father. Moreover, the Son is not a different person from
the Father simply because the Son has a father, whereas the
Father has no father. (For even if the Father had a father, He
Himself would still be different from the Son.) Likewise, the
Holy Spirit is not a different person from the Father simply
because, unlike the Father, the Holy Spirit proceeds from someone else. (For, even if the Father did proceed from someone else,
the Holy Spirit would still be different from the Father, from
whom He proceeds.) So it is clear that the Holy Spirit is not a
different person from the Father simply because the Spirit does
not have a son or a spirit proceeding from Himself, as the Father
does; nor is the Holy Spirit different from the Father simply
because He proceeds from another and the Father proceeds from
no one.

If the Holy Spirit does not exist from the Father, then He
cannot be understood to be a different person from the Father
solely on the basis of His being the spirit of the Father. For
someone can be understood to be different from another before
he is understood to be ''of'' that other—although he is unable
to be ''of another'' unless he is different. For example, when a
man is called the master or the servant of another man, he is
understood to be different from the one of whom he is said to be,
before he is understood to be his master or his servant. So,

therefore, if the Holy Spirit does not exist from the Father, nothing prohibits His being understood to be different from the Father before He is understood to be "of the Father." Hence, being the Father's spirit would not make Him different from the Father if He were not already different because He existed from the one whose spirit He is. Likewise, the Son is different from the Father—only because He exists by being begotten from the Father, whereby He is the Father's son.

Thus, it seems that the Holy Spirit is different from the Father only because He has His being-what-He-is from the Father—although His manner of being from the Father differs from that of the Son. Nevertheless, let us investigate this more thoroughly. Either the Holy Spirit became different from the Father after He became what He is or else the cause of this difference is in His very existing. For someone must exist before he can be different from another, and someone becomes different from another in existing. For it is impossible for anyone to be different before He exists. For example, the first man, before there was another man, was himself a man; but he was not "another man" until a second man came forth from him. For the first man became "another" as soon as he existed in relation to this second man. But the second man, who existed from the first, had his own existence and his "being another" simultaneously. Therefore, either the Holy Spirit was made different from the Father after He came into existence or else He has in His very existence the cause for being called different. But if He became different from the Father after He came into existence, then there were not always three persons—since the Holy Spirit could only be "another person" by being "an other" than the Father. So this would mean that, just as the Holy Spirit was not always different from the Father, so He (i.e., the Spirit of the Father) was not always a person. However, since these things are false, it is obvious that the Holy Spirit has in His very existence the cause for His being "another."

Now, the Holy Spirit can only have existence in one of two ways: (1) either from another (as is the case with the Son) or (2) from no one (as is the case with the Father). But if He exists from no one, then He exists just as the Father exists, and an alternative follows: Either (a) each one exists through Himself in such a way that neither has anything from the other; and then there are two gods, namely, the Father and the Holy Spirit. Or (b) since they are one God, and if each one exists from no one, then we are unable to find anything in the Christian faith to differentiate them from each other. But then the Father and the Holy Spirit would be one-and-the-same; i.e., they would both be one person. But true faith abhors both of these alternatives; therefore, it is certain that the Holy Spirit does not exist from no one. So, if He exists from another He exists from none other than God, who is Father, Son, and Holy Spirit. Now, in such case He cannot exist from Himself (a se ipso), since no person can originate from Himself. Hence, if someone denies that the Holy Spirit exists from the Son, then he must affirm that the Holy Spirit exists from the Father.

If someone says that the Holy Spirit does not exist from the Father, but that He can nevertheless be understood to be different from the Father by means of procession, then I think I must also reply to this, so that in this matter no possible objection to our assertion may go unanswered. Let no one marvel that I have tarried on this matter so long. For the Bishop of Bari was of no small authority among his own. Because he has failed to perceive that the Holy Spirit exists from the Father, and because I have not previously had the opportunity of responding, I have lingered on this topic. Now, whoever wants to deny that the Holy Spirit exists from the Father, but wants to maintain that the Holy Spirit is different from the Father by procession alone, understands this in one of two ways: (1) "to proceed" from the Father can mean "to be sent" or "to be given" by the Father; i.e., only when the Father sends or gives the Holy Spirit does the Holy Spirit proceed from the Father; or (2) "to proceed" can mean simply to exist from the Father. But if "to proceed" means "to be given" or "to be sent," then the Holy Spirit proceeds as much from the Son as from the Father. For the Son sends and gives Him as well as does the Father. And I think no one will argue that for the Holy Spirit "to proceed" means only that He is given or sent, for then He is different from the Father and proceeds from the Father only when He is given or sent. But the Holy Spirit is always different from the Father, even before there is a creature; yet He is only given or sent to a creature. And it must not be said that "to be given" or "to be sent" is something which *happens* to Him. For, since the Holy Spirit is omnipresent and immutable, something indeed happens to the creature receiving Him. As far as the creature is concerned, something happens which was not happening before and which is able not to happen. But with regard to the Holy Spirit, nothing happens which was not previously happening. For example, when a blind man who is in the light does not see the light, the light is not changing. But if the blind man sees the light after his blindness has been removed, then something happens to him, but nothing happens to the light. So we can conclude that the Holy Spirit is not different from the Father through procession when procession is understood in the sense of being given or sent. Hence, the alternative is clear, namely, that He proceeds from the Father in that He exists from the Father; and because He exists from the Father He is different from the Father. Likewise, the Son is different from the Father only because He exists from the Father. Therefore, the Holy Spirit is God from God and proceeds from God because He is God and because the Father from whom He is and proceeds is God.

Now, if we say that two processions of the Holy Spirit can be distinguished—one when He exists from the Father and the other when He is given or sent—then I do not think that this ought to be denied, provided that each procession is understood in its proper sense. For we can consistently interpret the following words of the Lord regarding that procession whereby the Holy Spirit is given or sent: "The wind blows wherever it will, and you hear the sound of it, but you do not know whence the wind comes or whither it goes" (John 3:8). This can be understood as follows: "You do not know whence the Holy Spirit proceeds or whither He recedes." For when the Spirit is given, He comes and proceeds as it were from concealment; and when He withdraws, He goes and recedes into concealment. Hence, it

can be said concerning *this* kind of procession that for the Holy
Spirit "to proceed" and "to be sent" signify the same thing.

Therefore, whether the Holy Spirit proceeds (1) only by
existing from the Father, or whether He proceeds (2) only when
He is given or sent in order to sanctify the creature, or whether
He proceeds (3) in both ways, it follows that He proceeds from
the Son. For (1) if He exists from the Father, He is God from
God; and we have already shown that in this case He also exists
and proceeds from the Son. For the Holy Spirit proceeds from
the one from whom He exists, and He exists from the one from
whom He proceeds. Or (2) if the Holy Spirit proceeds only by
being sent or given, then He proceeds from the Son, from whom
He is given and sent. And (3) if the Holy Spirit proceeds in
both ways, then we know [from the above] that He proceeds
from the Son in both ways. Therefore, we see that the Holy
Spirit is God from God and proceeds from God, even though this
is not stated in the aforementioned [Nicene-Constantinople]
Creed. Hence, if the Greeks deny that the Holy Spirit exists and
proceeds from the Son because the Creed is silent about this,
then they must also deny that He exists and proceeds from
God—something which is also not stated in the Creed. But if they
cannot deny that the Holy Spirit exists and proceeds from God,
then they should not fear (simply because they do not find this
formulated in the Creed) to confess with us that the Holy Spirit
exists and proceeds from the Son.

But the Greeks will say: "The Creed sufficiently signifies that
the Holy Spirit exists and proceeds from God when it states that
He proceeds from the Father, since the Father is God." To this
we respond with the same kind of argument: It is clearly
demonstrated that the Holy Spirit proceeds from the Son when
it is said that He proceeds from God, since the Son is God. Now,
I ask whether we should understand that (1) the Holy Spirit is
from the Father because He is from God or that (2) the Holy
Spirit is from God because He is from the Father? For, although
in each sentence the one fact is inferable from the other (for if
the Holy Spirit is from the Father, He is from God, and if He is
from God, He is from the Father—and nothing we have said

about the notion of relation contradicts this), nevertheless the one fact is not the *reason* for the other in both sentences [but only in one sentence]. For if the reason that the Holy Spirit exists from God is that He exists from the Father, then when it is said that He exists from the Father, we must not understand that He exists from that in virtue of which the Father is God, i.e., from the divine essence. Rather, we must understand that He exists from that in virtue of which God is the Father, i.e., from that in virtue of which He is referred to the Son. And then the divine essence in the Holy Spirit will not be from the deity of the Father but only from the relation of the Father. But this view is very foolish.

Even if someone wished to hold such a position, it would still follow that the Holy Spirit proceeds from the Son no less than from the Father. For there is no relation of father without a relation of son, just as the relation of son is nothing without the relation of father. Thus it will follow that the Holy Spirit exists from both of them if He exists from one of them. Therefore, if the Holy Spirit exists from the Father according to relation, He will also exist from the Son in the same way. But, since no one is really foolish enough to think this [viz., that the Holy Spirit does exist from the Father qua father], it must therefore be believed and confessed that the Holy Spirit exists from the Father *because* He exists from God. However, the Father is not more God than the Son, since Father and Son are one, unique, and true God. So then, if the Holy Spirit exists from the Father because He exists from God, who is the Father, then it cannot be denied that the Holy Spirit also exists from the Son since He exists from God, who is the Son.

CHAPTER III

Let us also consider what the Lord says in the Gospel: "And this is eternal life, that they know Thee the one true God, and Jesus Christ whom Thou hast sent" (John 17:3). The phrase "the one true God" must be understood in one of two ways.

First, "the one true God" may be taken to signify neither the Father alone nor the Son alone, but the Father and the Son at the same time. Or, second, "the one true God" can be taken to mean either the Father alone or the Son alone. But, if by naming the Father alone or the Son alone without adding the other name, we do not mean "the one true God," then neither the Father nor the Son is perfect God, but God is a composite of both Father and Son. But we believe that the Father is the perfect and one true God, and we believe the same thing about the Son. Hence, when we name either the Father alone or the Son alone, we mean nothing else than "the one true God," whom we know to be the same by both names (except for the relation by which they are referred to each other).

Therefore, when the Lord said, "This is eternal life, that they know Thee the one true God, and Jesus whom Thou hast sent," had He added "And the Holy Spirit proceeds from this one true God," then who would dare to separate the Son from that procession? For the one true God is neither more nor less the Father than the Son. Thus, if the one true God is meant when we name either the Father alone or the Son alone, or when we name both together, then what is more clear than that when the Holy Spirit is said to proceed from the Father, He is said to proceed from "the one true God," who is both Father and Son? For when the Son said that He and the Father are the one true God, if He had also added that the Holy Spirit proceeds from the one true God, then we would understand that the Holy Spirit proceeds from the Son. So also, when the Son says that the Holy Spirit proceeds from the Father, we clearly understand Him to mean that the Holy Spirit proceeds also from Himself.

Chapter IV

For the Lord Jesus speaks of "the Paraclete, the Holy Spirit, the one whom the Father will send in my name" (John 14:26); and He also speaks of the coming of the Paraclete, "whom I shall send to you from the Father" (John 15:26). How should the phrase "the one whom the Father will send in my name" be understood? Does this mean that the Holy Spirit will have the name of the Lord Jesus, so that when the Father sends the Holy Spirit this is the same as sending the Son? But the phrase "whom I shall send to you from the Father" cannot be interpreted in this sense, because the Son also sends the same Holy Spirit whom the Father sends, and the Son does not send the Son. Finally, we nowhere read in Scripture, and we absolutely deny, that the Holy Spirit is the Son. Thus, what else does "the one whom the Father will send in my name" mean besides this: that the one whom the Father will send, the Son also will send? Likewise, "whom I shall send from the Father" means only "the one whom I and the Father shall send." For "Son" is the name of the one who said, "The Father will send in my name." Hence, "the Father will send in my name" means nothing other than that the Father will send in the name of the Son. Therefore, what can "the Father will send in the name of the Son" mean except that the Father will send as if the Son were sending? Thereby, in the sending from the Father sending from the Son is understood. But how must we understand the phrase "the one whom I shall send from the Father"? Certainly the Holy Spirit is sent from the person from whom the Son sends Him. But the Son sends Him from the Father. Therefore, the Holy Spirit is sent from the Father. But that person sends from whom another is sent. Therefore, the Father is understood to send when the Son says: "I shall send from the Father." Therefore, what can "I shall send from the Father" mean except "I shall send as if the Father were sending—so that the Father's sending and my sending are one and the same"?

The Son is thus very careful to show that His own sending and that of the Father are one, so that the Father does not send except when the Son sends, nor does the Son send except when the Father sends. Hence, what does the Son wish to signify by His words, or what does He want to be understood, except that the Holy Spirit is not referred one way to the Father and another way to the Son and that He is not more the spirit of the one than of the other? For this reason, it is most difficult—

rather, it is impossible—to show that the Holy Spirit does not proceed from both. For how can both the Son and the Father give or send the Holy Spirit, and how can the Holy Spirit be the spirit of both if He does not exist from both together? For why does the Son give the Holy Spirit rather than the Holy Spirit give the Son, or why is the Holy Spirit "the Son's spirit" rather than the Son being "the Spirit's son" except for the fact that the Son is not from both the Father and the Holy Spirit together in the same way that the Holy Spirit is from both the Father and from the Son? For the Son is not given by the Holy Spirit, nor is He called the Spirit's son, since He does not exist from the Holy Spirit; and likewise, if the Holy Spirit were not from the Son, then He would not be given by the Son nor be called the Son's spirit. Now, the Greeks might say that the Holy Spirit does also send the Son, for it is said by the prophet, "and now the Lord God and His Spirit have sent me" (Is. 48:16). But this saying must be understood to refer to the humanity of the Son, who, when He was going to redeem the world, appeared in the world through the one will and ordinance (*dispositione*) of the Father and the Holy Spirit.

Nevertheless, I ask those who deny that the Holy Spirit both exists and proceeds from the Son, how they understand Him to be the spirit of the Son—since the Son sends Him as if He were His own spirit. Do they think that the Father gave the Son His own spirit as if giving to one who did not have a spirit from Himself? For the Son either has a spirit from Himself or from another. But if from another, this other would have to be the Father. In such case, the Son would have received a spirit from the Father (from whom He would have had the spirit); and the Father would have given the Holy Spirit to the Son as to one who did not have a spirit from Himself. Here the Greeks would have to show what cause there was, or what the Son's lack was, that the Father would give His spirit to the Son rather than giving His son to the Spirit—since the Father, the Son, and the Holy Spirit are all equal and each one is self-sufficient. Now, we do not deny that the Son has the Spirit from the Father in the following way: namely, that as the Son has His existence from the Father, so He also has from the Father the fact that a spirit exists from Himself, just as from the Father.[5] This is the case because the essence of the Father and of the Son is the same. But it is not the same thing to receive from the Father the essence from which the Holy Spirit proceeds as it is to receive the Holy Spirit from the Father. For when the Son is said to have from the Father the essence from which the Holy Spirit proceeds, no need is indicated in the Son. But when it is said that the Son receives from the Father the Holy Spirit, whom He does not have from Himself as the Father does, this seems to signify that the Son has something less than the Father and that the Holy Spirit is given to the Son as a supplement. But then it is not clear why the Son should need a holy spirit rather than the Holy Spirit needing a son. Someone might say to this that ''The Holy Spirit has been given to the Son so that when the Son gave the same Spirit, grace might be equally imputed to Him along with the Father.'' But this belief is earthly and very far from understanding deity—for it thinks of God assisting God as if He were needy, just as a man helps another man who is needy. For if the Father gives the Holy Spirit to the Son, God gives God to God. This is so because the Father is God, and the Son is God, and the Holy Spirit is God—all one and the same God. But we do not understand that God receives God from God except in the sense that God exists from God—as in the case of the Son and the Holy Spirit. Therefore, the Holy Spirit is said to be the spirit of the Son only because the Holy Spirit exists from the Son Himself.

CHAPTER V

We read that after the Resurrection the Lord breathed upon His disciples and said to them : ''Receive the Holy Spirit'' (John 20 :22). What does this inbreathing mean ? For we know that the

5. Cf. Augustine, *De Trinitate*, Bk. 15: Si enim quidquid habet, de Patre habet Filius; de Patre habet utique ut et de illo procedat Spiritus sanctus. Sed nulla ibi tempora cogitentur, quae habent prius et posterius: quia omnino nulla ibi sunt. PL, 42:1094.

breath which then proceeded from His mouth was not the Holy Spirit. And we do not believe that the inbreathing was done without signifying some mystery. Hence, what can be understood more rightly or appropriately here than that He did this so that we might understand that the Holy Spirit proceeds from Him? It is as if He had said, "Just as my breath proceeds from the depths of my body and my person, so (since sensible things can signify things which cannot be seen) the Holy Spirit, whom I signify to you by my breath, proceeds from the secret places of my deity and from my person." For we believe and confess that the Word and this man are one person, and that in the person there are two natures, namely, divine and human.

But perhaps the Greeks will argue as follows: "To be sure, the breath was not from the Lord's human substance, and yet the Lord breathed it out as if it were His own breath. Therefore, we are taught through the giving of the Holy Spirit in this manner that when the Son gives the Holy Spirit, He gives and sends His own Spirit, but not from His own divine essence." Hence, if there are any who hold this opinion, let them say that just as the breath is not the human nature when it is emitted from a man, so the Holy Spirit is not the divine substance when He is given or sent from God the Son. But no Christian can affirm this. And when those who make the above argument hear the words "The heavens have been established by the word of the Lord, and by the spirit of His mouth comes all their excellence" (Ps. 33:6), they deny that the phrase "spirit of His mouth" means the Holy Spirit. Let them also deny that the Holy Spirit is from the essence of the Lord, of whose mouth He is called the spirit. For the breath which usually proceeds from the mouth of men is not from the substance of the man who breathes it. But if they do not dare to deny that the Spirit of God is from the essence of God, and if they admit that the phrase "spirit of His mouth" symbolically signifies that the Holy Spirit proceeds from the depths of God's essence (of whose mouth He is called the Spirit), then let them also confess that the same Holy Spirit proceeds from the essence of the Son, of whose lips He is called the Spirit. For in the prophet we read concerning Christ that

"by the spirit of His lips He will slay the wicked" (Is. 11:4).
Therefore, either our opponents must argue that there is a
difference between "the spirit of His mouth" and "the spirit of
His lips" (which cannot be done) or else they must concede that
the Holy Spirit proceeds alike from the Father, of whose mouth
He is called the Spirit, and from the Son, of whose lips He is
called the Spirit.

But if they say that the "spirit of His lips" does not mean the
Holy Spirit, but rather means the words of the Lord's preaching
which He formed by the air of His breath in a human way, and
by which words and teaching He slays the wicked man by avert-
ing him from wickedness—then they are wrong. For neither
audible words nor a breath of air does this, but only the Holy
Spirit, about whom God says through the prophet, "I will take
out of your flesh the heart of stone and give you a heart of flesh.
And I will put my spirit within you" (Ez. 36:26–27). Therefore,
the Holy Spirit slays the wicked when He converts his heart
from wickedness to reverence. And if by this wicked one we
understand the Antichrist, "whom the Lord Jesus will slay by
the spirit of His mouth" (II Thess. 2:8), then I do not think
that anyone will attribute that power so much to the breath of
the human voice as to the divine Spirit.

Therefore, if we understand the Holy Spirit to be referred to
in these sayings—namely, (1) when He is called the spirit of the
mouth of the Lord, by whose word the heavens have been established (i.e., He is the Spirit of the Father); and (2) when He is
called the spirit of the mouth of the Lord Jesus and (3) the
spirit of His lips—then there is no reason why the Holy Spirit
ought to be understood to proceed more from the mouth of the
Father than from the mouth of the Son. And we may understand
"mouth of the Father" to mean "essence of the Father," for
His mouth is not different from His essence; for just as the
"word of the Lord" is from His essence, so the "spirit of His
mouth" can only be from His essence. And if this is so, then
what is more obvious than that the spirit of the mouth and lips
of the Son exists and proceeds from the essence of the Son—just
as the spirit of the Father's mouth exists and proceeds from the

essence of the Father? For, take this text: "The heavens have been established by the word of the Lord, and by the spirit of His mouth comes all their excellence" (Ps. 33:6). I do not think that anyone will construe this verse as referring merely to transitory words or will understand "spirit" here to refer to the breath of air which after being inhaled is emitted through the mouth of the speaker. But, however anyone might desire to interpret these texts, it is sufficient that the breathing of the Lord upon His disciples (which I have already mentioned) was done to signify that the Spirit whom He gave was proceeding from the mystery of His person, from whose hiddenness was proceeding that Spirit which He was breathing forth. Finally, when the divine Scripture signifies some mystery through the likeness of sensible things, the things which signify cannot be completely similar to those things which are signified. For this would not be a likeness but an identity, unless perhaps someone wishes to say that the breathing forth was done simply by the wisdom of God without any spiritual significance. But I do not think that anyone is so unperceptive as to believe this.

CHAPTER VI

The Son also says about the Holy Spirit: "For He will not speak on His own authority, but whatsoever He will hear that shall He speak" (John 16:13). But what does His not speaking on His own authority mean except that He will have from another that which He will speak? And what does His having from another that which He shall speak mean except that He will have from another the knowledge of those things which He shall speak? Thus, after the Son says of the Holy Spirit, "He will not speak on His own authority," He then adds, "but whatsoever He will hear that shall He speak." What does "hearing" mean for the Holy Spirit except, as it were, "learning," and what does "learning" mean except "receiving knowledge"? If, therefore, the Holy Spirit's knowledge is not different from His essence, then He has His essence from the person from whom He hears those things which He speaks and which He teaches. For it is the same for the Holy Spirit to speak as to teach. But He neither hears nor has His essence from anyone other than the Father or the Son. But if He exists from the Father, then, according to the argument previously given, He also exists from the Son. This is why the Son also says the same thing about the Holy Spirit when He states: "He will glorify me because He will take what is mine and will declare it unto you" (John 16:14). For what else does this mean except that "He will hear from me (i.e., He will know from me) that which He will declare unto you"? When the Son said, "Whatsoever He will hear that shall He speak," He did not designate the one from whom the Holy Spirit would hear. But when He says, "He will take what is mine," then so that no one should attribute to the Father alone that which the Holy Spirit hears from another, He shows clearly that it is from Him as well as from the Father that the Holy Spirit receives His knowledge, or essence. When the Lord Jesus says of the Holy Spirit, "He will not speak on His own authority, but whatsoever He will hear that shall He speak and declare unto you," this signifies that the Holy Spirit exists and proceeds from the one from whom He hears. Thus, when the Son asserts that "He will take what is mine and declare it unto you," the Son clearly shows that the Holy Spirit has His essence from, and proceeds from, the Son's own essence. For what is not the divine essence is inferior to the Holy Spirit. And the Holy Spirit does not receive from the Son something which it is beneath Him to receive. Therefore, when the Son says, "He will take what is mine," this signifies nothing other than the Son's own essence.

CHAPTER VII

Perhaps our opponents will try to understand the Son's statement about the Holy Spirit—"He will receive from me and declare unto you"—differently from the way I have interpreted it. But what will they say about this text: "No one knows the Son except the Father, or the Father except the Son and anyone to whom the Son chooses to reveal Him'' (Matt. 11:27)? We hear that no one knows the Father or the Son except the Father or the Son, and the one to whom the Son reveals this knowledge. The Lord does not say ''no one'' in the sense of ''no man,'' but as if He had said ''absolutely no one.'' For if He had intended the former, He would not have added, ''except the Father,'' because the Father is not a man. And when He says, ''No one knows the Father,'' ''no one'' refers not simply to human persons but to all persons. Therefore, absolutely no one has this knowledge except the Father and the Son and the one to whom the Son reveals this knowledge. Hence, either the Holy Spirit does not know the Father and the Son (a thought which is impious) or else the Son reveals to the Holy Spirit the knowledge of Himself and of the Father. This knowledge is nothing other than the essence of the Holy Spirit.

Now, they might argue as follows: ''Although the Son, in so far as it pertains to the wording of this text, does not concede this knowledge to anyone except to Himself, to the Father, and to anyone to whom the Son reveals this knowledge; nevertheless, it must not be admitted that the Holy Spirit is separated from this knowledge, or that He receives it from the Son. For the Father and the Son know themselves only through their being one with the Holy Spirit. And therefore, when the Son says that the Father and the Son know each other, the Holy Spirit must also be understood to share in this knowledge. And so when the Son reveals this knowledge, He reveals it not to the Holy Spirit but to a creature.'' Now, if someone argues in this way, then we immediately and firmly proceed as follows: Though Truth Himself—even on their interpretation of His words—denies that the Holy Spirit knows the Father and the Son unless the Son reveals this knowledge to the Spirit, our opponents argue that we ought not attend to the words so much as to the notion of God's unity of essence, which is one and inseparable in all three persons. But if so, then (I say) we ought still more to heed the previously discussed consequence which follows from this unity—since no oral or written authority denies it, nor affirms anything that is contradictory or in any way repugnant to our position.

If the Greeks are unwilling openly to resist the truth, they must choose one of two alternatives: either (1) the Holy Spirit does not know the Father and the Son unless the Son reveals this knowledge or (2) since the Father and the Son in their knowing each other are one with the Holy Spirit when they are said to know themselves, it necessarily follows that the Holy Spirit is understood to share in that same knowledge. For there is no way to avoid these alternatives if they are unwilling completely to take away this knowledge from the Holy Spirit or to take away the truth from the words of Truth Himself. But denying such knowledge or truth is repugnant to true faith, for the Truth speaks as follows: "No one knows the Son except the Father, or the Father except the Son and any one to whom the Son chooses to reveal Him." So if the Greeks choose the first alternative, which asserts that the Holy Spirit knows the Father and the Son through the revelation of the Son, then the Holy Spirit has this knowledge from the Son, and this is the same as for Him to have existence from the Son. Therefore, the Holy Spirit exists and proceeds from the Son, since He proceeds from the one from whom He exists. And if they choose the second alternative, they assert that when the Father and the Son are said to know themselves, the essence through which they know themselves is the same for the Holy Spirit, so that the Holy Spirit shares the same knowledge. Hence when they read that the Holy Spirit proceeds from the Father, about whom the Son says, "I and the Father are one" (John 10:30), then let them confess with us that because of the essential identity of Father and Son the Holy Spirit also doubtless proceeds from the Son.

CHAPTER VIII

Now, the Greeks may oppose our saying that the Son is begotten from the Father and that the Holy Spirit proceeds from the Father and the Son by arguing that this establishes grades of dignity or intervals in eternity—as if the Holy Spirit could not exist until the Son had first been begotten from the Father. This, they say, would make the Holy Spirit exist later than the Son. So they might argue that it is more correct to say that the Son and the Holy Spirit equally exist from the Father, just as brightness and heat come simultaneously from the sun. And just as the brightness is not from the heat, nor the heat from the brightness, so the Son exists from the Spirit by proceeding—in such a way that neither the Son exists from the Spirit nor the Spirit from the Son. So if someone should propose this objection to our position, then we would respond as follows: we do not attribute grades of dignity to God, who is one; nor do we establish intervals in eternity (i.e., in that which is beyond all time) when we affirm the Son's existing from the Father, or the Holy Spirit's existing from the Father and the Son. Similarly, all of us who hold the Christian faith confess the Son to be neither less nor later than the Father, although the Son has existence only from Him. In the same way, we do not confess that the Holy Spirit is less or later than the Son when we say that He exists or proceeds from the Son. For certainly, although brightness and heat proceed from the sun and cannot exist without a sun from which to proceed, nevertheless we know that there is no earlier and later in these three, viz., the sun, its brightness, and its heat. And if this is true in these temporal things, then how much less can the three persons of the Trinity be understood to be susceptible of intervals in their existence; for they exist in eternity, where there are no temporal limitations.

Moreover, our opponents cannot rightly maintain that the Son and the Holy Spirit can exist from the Father alone, so that neither Son nor Holy Spirit exists from the other—much as brightness and heat proceed together from the sun, so that neither exists from the other. For when we say that the Son and the Holy Spirit both exist from the Father, we confess that God the Son and God the Holy Spirit both exist from God the Father; and we confess that these three persons are one God, and that this very God exists from Himself. But in the case of the sun, we do not say that the sun exists from the sun when brightness and heat exist from the sun; nor do we say that the brightness and heat which exist from the sun are also the sun, nor that the three are one sun. For if either the heat and the sun or the brightness and the sun were one sun, then it would be necessary either that the brightness be from the heat (since brightness would exist from the whole sun, which would be the same thing as heat) or that heat be from brightness (since heat would exist from the sun, which would not differ in essence from brightness).

Nevertheless, let us suppose that the Son and the Spirit exist equally from the Father alone, just as heat and brightness exist from the sun alone. Then on what grounds do those who say this confess that the Holy Spirit is the Son's spirit while denying that the Son is the Spirit's son? For just as there is no reason for granting that the heat is the brightness' heat or that the brightness is the heat's brightness, so truth does not allow that the Holy Spirit is the Son's spirit rather than the Son being the Spirit's son. So then, if they cannot bring themselves to deny that the Holy Spirit is the Son's spirit, then let them deny that the Son and the Holy Spirit exist equally from the Father alone, in the way that brightness and heat exist from one sun. Wherefore, if the Greeks object to our position by arguing from this example of the heat and brightness of the sun, the argument will work neither for them nor against us.

CHAPTER IX

Now, in order not to separate the Son altogether from the communion of the Father in this procession of the Holy Spirit, the Greeks say, as we are told, that the Holy Spirit proceeds from the Father *through* the Son (*per filium*). But it is not clear how this is to be understood, especially since they find no texts by which to prove it clearly. They may suppose themselves to be supported by that Scripture which says about God that "all things are from Him, through Him, and in Him" (Rom. 11:36). If they understand by this verse that all things are from the one who is the Father and through the one who is the Son and in the one who is the Holy Spirit, then we fully agree that all things are from the Father, through the Son, and in the Holy Spirit. But if they understand the Apostle's words to assert that the Holy Spirit Himself is included among all those things which exist through the Son, then they are making too fine a distinction. For it is impossible to assert that any one of the three persons is among all those things and to exclude the other two. Because if Father, Son, and Holy Spirit are included among all the things which the Apostle says are *from* the Father, *through* the Son, and *in* the Holy Spirit, then a rational mind can see how much confusion such an assertion would lead to. Therefore, without doubt, we should understand the Apostle's saying that "all things are from Him, through Him, and in Him" to refer to all the things created by God; for these created things are from Him, and through Him, and in Him—as one thing is from another, through another, and in another. For whatever has been created is not the same as God, but is something different from Him. But the Holy Spirit is not something different from God; rather He is the same God as the Father and the Son.

Now, clearly, there is no other way for them to show that the Holy Spirit proceeds, as they say, from the Father through the Son. For the Father and the Son do not differ in the unity of deity, nor does the Holy Spirit proceed from the Father except it be from His deity. Therefore, if the Son has the same deity as the Father, it is impossible to understand how the Holy Spirit proceeds from the deity of the Father *through* the deity of the Son, but not *from* the deity of the Son. Perhaps someone might suggest that the Holy Spirit does not proceed from the deity of the Father but rather proceeds from His paternity, or that the Holy Spirit does not proceed through the deity of the Son but through his sonship. But such an opinion is so obviously foolish that it stifles itself.

Some may object when I say that the Holy Spirit proceeds from the deity of the Father and from the deity of the Son. They may argue that I am thus unable to distinguish the deity of the Holy Spirit from the deity of the Father and of the Son since the deity of the three is one and the same. Thus, they think to conclude against me that if the Holy Spirit proceeds from the deity of the Father and of the Son, then He also proceeds from His own deity; and on that account the Holy Spirit is said to proceed from Himself. But I recall having sufficiently replied to this above, showing that no person is able to exist from Himself (*ex se*). For just as the Son does not exist from Himself but from the Father alone, when He exists from the essence of the Father and has the same essence as the Father, so the Holy Spirit does not exist from Himself but from the Father and the Son, when He exists from the essence of the Father and of the Son and has the same essence as the Father and the Son.

The Greeks will say: "Why are we not able to assert that the Holy Spirit proceeds from the Father through the Son just as we say that all things have been created by the Father through the Word, who is the Son? For when the Father created through His Word, He did not create through something other than that which He Himself is; i.e., He did not create by something other than His essential power, which is the same power as that of the Word. Nevertheless, He is said to create through the Word. So why do we not say as well that the Holy Spirit proceeds from the Father through the Word, since the Holy Spirit does not proceed from the Father except from that essence and through that essence which is the same in the Father as in the Son, although the Spirit proceeds not as a creature, but as God proceeding from God?"

Let us see what follows if we say this; and then let there be peace between us. It is certain that what has been created by the Father through the Word has been created as well by the Word itself. For that very Word says: "Whatever the Father does, this the Son does likewise" (John 5:19). Therefore, since the Holy Spirit proceeds from the Father through the Son, let us say likewise that He proceeds *from* the Son—just as everything which was created by the Father *through* the Word likewise was created *by* the Word itself. Of course, they may understand the Holy Spirit to proceed from the Father through the Son in the same way that a spring flows into a river and the river is collected into a lake, so that the lake is said to be from the spring through the river. But here the river is not in the spring, but rather outside the spring; whereas the Son is in the Father and not outside the Father. Therefore, the Holy Spirit is not from the Father through the Son in the same way that a lake is from a spring through a river. Nevertheless, even if the comparison did hold, still we could not deny that the Holy Spirit is from the Son, although He is as well from the Father through the Son—even as we must admit that a lake is from a river, even though it is from a spring through a river. If anyone denies that a lake exists from a river simply because the river is first from a spring, then let him also say that he was not begotten of his own father but only from Adam, because he is from Adam through his father. Let him say too that the Son of the Virgin is not from Mary, nor from David, nor from Abraham, because these first came into existence by being begotten from Adam. And let such a man deny the truth of what was said to Abraham, to David, and to Mary. To Abraham is said, "In your seed shall all nations be blessed" (Gen. 22:18); and to David is said, "From the fruit of your loins I will raise one to your throne" (Ps. 132:11); and to Mary is said, "Blessed is the fruit of your womb" (Luke 1:42). So such a person would have to say that Christ is not the seed or fruit of Abraham, David, and Mary, but rather is of the seed of Adam—since all of these have descended from Adam. But according to this interpretation the one who is the Son of the Virgin is not from Adam either, but rather is from the clay from which Adam was made.

Yet the Greeks will insist: "It is proper for us to say that the Holy Spirit does not proceed from the Son but from the Father through the Son, although He is from the Father and from the Son in the same way that the lake is from the spring and from the river. The dispute between us concerns the meaning of the word 'procession'; for you assert, and we deny, that the Holy Spirit proceeds from the Son. Look at the river: You can see it proceeding from the spring as if from its source of origin. But a lake does not proceed from a river, even though it exists from a river; rather, it is collected from a river. Therefore, even if the Holy Spirit has His existence from the Son, nevertheless He is not properly said to proceed from the Son, but to proceed from the Father—His source of origin (*originali principio*), as it were."

This reasoning would perhaps be proper if the Son's being born from the Father implied a procession outside the Father. Then after a certain interval the Holy Spirit might be understood to be from the Father before He is from the Son, just as the river flowing from the spring proceeds outside the spring and after a certain interval in time and space is collected into a lake. So the lake is first from the spring before it is from the river; and thus it is from the spring and through the river rather than from the river and through the spring. But since the Son, being begotten from the Father, does not go beyond the Father but remains in Him, He is not different from the Father in regard either to place or time or essence. And since that from which the Holy Spirit proceeds is one and the same with the Father and the Son, we cannot understand, nor ought we say, that the Holy Spirit proceeds from the Father but not from the Son. Thus, we cannot see what reason the Greeks have for saying that the Holy Spirit does not proceed from the Son, but from the Father through the Son. For even if the Holy Spirit proceeds through the Son, it cannot be denied that He also exists from the Son.

Now, someone might wish to argue that just as a river seems more properly to proceed from a spring than a lake to proceed from a river, so it is more proper to say that the Son proceeds from the Father than that the Holy Spirit proceeds from the Son—even though the Holy Spirit exists from the Son. By this reasoning he might avoid conceding that the Holy Spirit proceeds from the Son, from whom He exists in the same way that a lake exists from a river. But we do not deny that one who is begotten proceeds in some way from the one from whom he is begotten; and we affirm that the Holy Spirit proceeds in His own way, though not, as it were, from two springs, but truly from one spring, and in such a way that the procession of the Son does not lose the name "Begotten" and the procession of the Holy Spirit does not receive it. Therefore, there is no reason why it should be said that the Son proceeds from the Father more than the Holy Spirit proceeds from the Son.

Let us more diligently consider, so that we may know that the Holy Spirit exists from both the Father and the Son, how a lake exists from a spring and from a river equally. For through the consideration of this temporal and spatial thing we can understand what is eternal. As I have written to Pope Urban (of venerable memory) in my epistle *On the Incarnation of the Word,* there are many things in the consideration of the lake, the spring, and the river that bear a suitable likeness to the one God and the three persons. It is evident that one and the same water is in the spring, in the river, and in the lake. So there are not three waters—although the spring, the river, and the lake are three things. Let us, then, distinguish between the spring, the river, and the lake; and let us see how these individual things— although they are three—are understood to be one water. In the spring the water bubbles up from the depths; in the river it flows down from the spring; in the lake it is collected and remains. Therefore, "spring" indicates water bubbling up from a spring; "river" refers to water flowing forth from the spring; and "lake" indicates water being collected together. So we see that a river does not come from that with respect to which water is called a spring; but it comes from that which it is, viz., water. Nor does a lake come from that with respect to which water is called a spring or a river, but it comes from water itself—which is one and the same in both a spring and a river. Therefore, a lake does not exist from that which differentiates a spring and a river, but from that in which they are one. If, therefore, the spring is not more that from which the lake exists than the river is, then the lake cannot be understood to be from the spring more than from the river. Thus, when the Father or the Son or the Holy Spirit is called God, we understand in the three one essence and one God, since "God" is the name which signifies that essence. However, by "Father," the one begetting is understood; by "Son," the one begotten is understood; and by "Holy Spirit," the one who proceeds in a certain unique and ineffable way is understood. Therefore, just as the lake does not exist from that in virtue of which the spring and the river are different from each other, but rather from the water which they have in common, so the Holy Spirit does not exist from that in virtue of which the Father and the Son are different from each other, but rather from the divine essence in which they are one. If, therefore, the Father is not more the essence from which the Holy Spirit exists than is the Son, it cannot be understood why the Holy Spirit should exist more from the Father than from the Son.

Chapter X

Now, the Greeks might say that the Holy Spirit cannot exist from two causes or from two sources (*principiis*). We reply that just as we do not believe the Holy Spirit exists from that in virtue of which the Father and the Son are two different persons, but exists from that in virtue of which they are one, so we do not speak of two sources of His existence, but only of one source. For when we say that God is the source of the creature, we understand Father, Son, and Holy Spirit to be one source and not three; for there is but one creator and not three creators. And although the Father, the Son, and the Holy Spirit are three, yet when we speak of the Father, or the Son, or the Holy Spirit as Source or Creator we refer to that in virtue of which all three are one and not to that in virtue of which they are three. Therefore, although the Father is Source and the Son is Source and the Holy Spirit is Source, nevertheless they are not three sources but one. So when the Holy Spirit is said to exist from the Father and from the Son, He does not exist from two sources but from one, which is Father and Son together, just as He exists from one God, who is both Father and Son—if it is proper to say that God has a source, or cause.

Now "source" seems to refer to a thing's beginning, and "cause" seems to refer to an effect. But the Holy Spirit never begins to be; nor is He the effect of anything. For what begins to be advances from not-being into being; and the term "effect" seems properly to be applied to that which comes to be. Nevertheless, since it is true that the Son is from the Father, and since the Holy Spirit is from the Father and from the Son, there is a sense in which it can be properly said that the Father is the source of the being of the Son and that the Father and the Son are the source of the being of the Holy Spirit—so long as this is understood in a certain ineffable way which cannot be otherwise expressed. However, we do not confess two sources, viz., the Father of the Son, and the Father and the Son of the Holy Spirit; nor do we believe that the Father from whom the Son exists is one God and that the Father and Son from whom the Holy Spirit exists is another God—although Son and Holy Spirit exist from the same source, or from the same God, according to their own manner of being. This means that the Son exists by being begotten and that the Holy Spirit exists by proceeding—as long as this procession is understood in a unique and ineffable way. For procession is spoken of in many ways; but the procession of the Holy Spirit is understood as unique, just as the begetting of the Son is understood as unique. Therefore, we understand the same thing if we say that the Father is the cause of the Son or that the Father and Son are the cause of the Holy Spirit. Now, in saying this we cannot speak of two causes, viz., one of the Son and one of the Holy Spirit; for there are not two gods. There is only one God and only one cause of the existence of both the Son and the Holy Spirit.

CHAPTER XI

The Lord spoke of the coming of the Paraclete, "the Spirit of Truth, who proceeds from the Father" (John 15:26). Now, someone might ask why the Lord did not add "and from the Son" or "from me" if He had wished this addition to be understood. If this be asked, I reply that it is not unusual for the Lord to attribute something to the Father as if to Him alone, or to attribute something to Himself alone or to the Holy Spirit alone, so that whatever is said of one is understood to pertain to the others as well. For when He says "Blessed are you, Simon bar Jona, because flesh and blood have not revealed this to you, but my Father who is in heaven" (Matt. 16:17), should not the Son Himself and the Holy Spirit be understood to have revealed this to Peter together with the Father? For since the Father does not reveal with respect to the fact that He is the Father but with respect to the fact that He is God, and since God Himself is Son and Holy Spirit as well, it follows that whatever the Father reveals, the Son and the Holy Spirit also reveal.

Likewise when the Lord says, "No one knows the Son except the Father, nor the Father except the Son and anyone to whom the Son chooses to reveal Him" (Matt. 11:27), it seems as though only the Son knows and reveals the Father and Himself, and as though only the Father knows the Son. But it must be understood here that revealing and knowing are common to the three persons because they know and reveal not with respect to the fact that they are different from one another but with respect to the fact that they are one God. For when He says that the Father knows the Son and the Son knows the Father and reveals both Himself and the Father, it is clear that He wants it to be understood that the Father knows the Holy Spirit and that the Son knows and reveals the Holy Spirit, since that which the Father and the Son are the Holy Spirit also is.

Similarly, when the Lord says, "Whoever sees me sees the Father also" (John 14:9), it ought not be thought that the Holy Spirit is excluded, since whoever sees that in virtue of which the Father and Son and Holy Spirit are one cannot see one of the three without seeing the other two. And He also speaks to the apostles about the Holy Spirit, saying, "When the Spirit of Truth comes, He will teach you all truth" (John 16:13)—as if only the Holy Spirit would teach all truth (although He does not teach all truth without the Father and the Son). But it is not with respect to the fact that the Holy Spirit is the Spirit of someone (viz., of the Father and of the Son), but with respect to the fact that He is one with the Father and the Son, i.e., with respect to the fact that He is God, that the Holy Spirit teaches all truth.

Can you not see, therefore, how in the things I have set forth, what is attributed as if to one person alone cannot be separated from the other two persons? We find many texts of this sort in the Holy Scriptures, wherein what is said of one person singularly is understood of all three persons equally. For whatever is spoken concerning one person ought to be understood of the others equally—except when the fact that they are different from one another is known to oppose this (as I have explained previously). Now, we believe that the Holy Spirit proceeds from the Father, since God exists from God—i.e., since the essence of the Holy Spirit exists from the essence of the Father, there being one essence in three persons. And since we believe this, it is necessary—if the Son does not exist from the Holy Spirit—that we also confess that the Holy Spirit exists from the Son. For the Holy Spirit exists from that which the Son is and that which the Father also is.

But someone will say: "We also understand the Son and the Holy Spirit to reveal what the Father alone is said to reveal; and we understand the Father and the Holy Spirit to reveal and to know what the Son alone is said to do; and we understand the Father and the Son to teach what only the Holy Spirit alone is promised to be going to teach. We think this because what we read about one person alone in one place is clearly signified elsewhere concerning the others. But, while Scripture says that the Holy Spirit proceeds from the Father, we do not read anywhere that He proceeds also from the Son. By this we are warned not to assert on our own opinion, or authority, that which is nowhere stated in Scripture."

We reply that through those things which are said we are taught to understand in a like way those things which occur in like sayings, even when such things are left unsaid—and all the more so when we see that these things which are left unsaid clearly follow by rational necessity from those things which are said, and that there is no opposing reason. For when the Lord says to the Father, "This is life eternal, that they know Thee, the one true God, and Jesus Christ, whom Thou hast sent" (John 17:3), ought we to deny that knowledge of the Holy Spirit is also life-giving and health-giving, and deny it simply because Scripture nowhere says: "This is life eternal, that they know the Father, the one true God, and the Holy Spirit," or "This is life eternal, that they know the Son, the one true God, and the Holy Spirit"? Or when we read that "just as the Father has life in Himself, so He has granted the Son also to have life in Himself" (John 5:26), shall we say that the Holy Spirit does not have in Himself life from the Father from whom He exists (as the Father and the Son have life in themselves) simply because the Son nowhere says this about the Holy Spirit as He does about Himself? Or when the Son says, "The Father is in me and I am in the Father" (John 14:10, 11) and "Whoever sees me sees the Father also" (John 14:9), are we going to deny that the Holy Spirit is in the Father and in the Son, and that the Father and the Son are in the Holy Spirit? Or shall we deny that he who sees the Son also sees the Holy Spirit as well as the Father—basing our denial on the fact that these things are not read in a text which affirms them with respect to the Father and the Son?

Rather, since the Father, the Son, and the Holy Spirit are one and the same God, then when it is said that to know the one true God (Father and Son) is to have eternal life, the Holy Spirit ought to be included inseparably as an object of that knowledge. And when we read that "just as the Father has life in Himself, so He has granted the Son also to have life in Himself," we should not judge that this life is foreign to the Holy Spirit or that He does not have life in Himself. And when we hear, "The Father is in me and I am in the Father" and "Whoever sees me sees the Father also," we ought to know by these things which are said that the Holy Spirit is not outside the Father and the Son, nor the Father and the Son outside the Holy Spirit; and we should know that in seeing the Son, the Holy Spirit as well as the Father is seen. For just as the Father is not one God, and the Son another God, and the Holy Spirit a third God, so too God does not have anything in Himself other than God, nor is God outside God, nor is God dissimilar to God.

Finally, where in the Prophets, in the Gospels, or in the Apostles do we read in just so many words that the one God exists in three persons, or that the one God is a Trinity, or that God is from God? Nor do we encounter the words "person" and "trinity" in that Creed in which the procession of the Holy Spirit from the Son is also not set forth. Nevertheless, since these things clearly follow from those things which we do read, we steadfastly believe them in our hearts and confess them with our mouths. Therefore, we ought to receive with certainty not only whatever we read in the Holy Scriptures but also whatever follows from Scripture by rational necessity—as long as there is no reason against it.

CHAPTER XII

Although the things which have already been said above can suffice, nevertheless I shall add something more to them to show that the Holy Spirit exists from the Son. The Greeks confess with us that the Holy Spirit is the Spirit of God, and the Spirit of the Father, and the Spirit of the Son. I ask, therefore, whether they understand Him to be the Spirit of God, and the Spirit of the Father, and the Spirit of the Son all in the same way or in dissimilar ways? It is certain that the Holy Spirit is not called the Spirit of God in the sense of possession—as, for example, when we speak of the horse of someone or the house of someone. For the one who possesses is greater than that which is possessed. But God is not greater than the Holy Spirit—because the Holy Spirit is God, and God cannot be greater than God. Nor is the Holy Spirit called the Spirit of God in the sense of being a member of God, as, for example, when we speak of the hand or foot of a man. For God does not have any members or any parts. How, therefore, can the Holy Spirit be understood to be the Spirit of God except in the sense that what He is, He is from God? For the name ''Father'' does not signify anything other than God who exists as Father, or God in relation to the Son, from which relation He derives the name ''Father.'' And we ought to speak similarly of the Son. For nothing is understood by the name ''Son'' other than God who exists as Son, or the relation by which He is referred to the Father and through which He is called Son. But no one with understanding thinks that the Holy Spirit is the Spirit of the Father or the Spirit of the Son with respect to the fact that the Father and the Son are different from each other, but only with respect to the fact that both are one and the same God. For this reason one and the same thing is meant when the Spirit of God is called the "Spirit of the Father" and the "Spirit of the Son."

But the Holy Spirit is called the Spirit of God and the Spirit of the Father because He exists and proceeds from God and from the Father. And so He also exists and proceeds from the Son since He is called, in the same sense, the Spirit of the Son. For if when the Holy Spirit is called "Spirit of God" and "Spirit of the Lord," we do not understand "Spirit of the Son" in the same sense as "Spirit of the Father," then we face two alternatives: either we shall exclude the Son from the name "God" or from the name "Lord"; or else we must understand that the Spirit of God or the Spirit of the Lord is twofold. But whence do the Greeks get that opinion? Where does Scripture say that when we read the words "the Spirit of God" or "the Spirit of the Lord" these words should not be understood in the same way concerning the Father and concerning the Son? Or where is anything found from which this follows? The Greeks may say, "When the Holy Spirit is called the Spirit of the Father, two senses are understood: He is the Spirit of the Father both because He exists from the Father and because He is given by the Father; but He is the Spirit of the Son only because He is given by the Son." But this is precisely the view for which I am asking a justification. And if they admit that this view is stated in no authentic text and that it does not follow from that which has been written, why then do they censure us for saying that the Holy Spirit proceeds from the Son even though these very words cannot be read in Scripture. For we understand this conclusion to follow necessarily from that which they themselves read and believe.

Therefore, let our opponents themselves judge which of the following alternatives ought to be adopted, even though Scripture is silent concerning both: should we adopt what we say— namely, that the Holy Spirit proceeds from the Son, a fact which we can demonstrate to follow from those things which we truly believe; or should we adopt what they say—namely, that the

Holy Spirit is in one way the Spirit of the Father and in another way that of the Son, something which they can demonstrate by no authority or no reason, and something which they cannot show to follow from those things which are certain? Indeed, they certainly ought to do one of two things: either they ought to give up their opinion that the Holy Spirit is in one way the Spirit of the Son and in another way the Spirit of the Father (if, as I hear, this is their opinion), since they nowhere read this in Scripture and cannot prove it; or at least they ought not to censure us for saying that the Holy Spirit proceeds from the Son, although we do not read these words anywhere in Scripture either—since we show that this conclusion follows from those things which we believe equally with the Greeks. But if they give up their opinion, then let them believe equally with us that the Holy Spirit is the Spirit of the Father and in like manner is the Spirit of the Son; and let them understand that He proceeds from the Son just as He proceeds from the Father. And if they cease censuring us, then let them confess with us that doctrine for which they know we should not be censured.

Chapter XIII

But now we must consider their criticism of us for adding to the Creed (which they hold and affirm together with us) that the Holy Spirit proceeds from the Son. For they ask why this addition was made and why it was not first shown to their church so that what was to be added might have been considered together with us and added by common consent. To this question we have a sufficient response. For, if they ask why this addition was made, we answer that it was necessary on account of certain men, lacking understanding, who were not aware of what is contained among the things which the universal church believes, and who did not know that it follows from these beliefs that the Holy Spirit proceeds from the Son. Thus, the addition was made so that such men should not hesitate to believe this doctrine. We can see how needful this addition was from the fact that the

Greeks reject the doctrine simply because it was not inserted into the Creed. Therefore, since there was such need and since there was no reason against it nor any incompatibility with true faith, the Latin Church faithfully asserted what it knew had to be believed and confessed. For we know that not everything which we ought to believe and confess is stated in this Creed. Nor did those who formulated the Creed want Christians to be satisfied to confess and believe only those things which they laid down. For example, to mention only one case, it is not said in this Creed that the Lord descended into Hell. Nevertheless, both we and the Greeks believe this. And if they say that a creed which is regarded with such great authority ought in no way to be corrupted, we ourselves do not judge it to be a corruption where we add nothing to the Creed which is contrary to those things said in it. And, although we are able to defend this addition as not being a corruption, we reply to those who would obstinately accuse us of corrupting the Creed, that we have not corrupted it but have only formulated something new. For we preserve and venerate with the Greeks the whole of that Creed which has been translated literally from the Greek language; however, we have added the aforesaid phrase to this Creed, which we use regularly in the hearing of the people; and this use is in accordance with the Latin custom.

Now, as to the question why this addition was made without seeking the agreement of the Greek Church, we answer that it was extremely difficult for the Latins to gather the Greek bishops for consultation concerning this matter. Nor was it necessary to raise the question in the Latin Church, where there was no doubt about it. For what church, even though extended throughout a single kingdom, is not entitled to establish something to be read and to be sung in the hearing of the people, as long as what is established accords with right faith?[6] So is it not all the more permitted to the Latin Church to propose that which all the nations and kingdoms that use the Latin language agree upon?

6. Anselm here witnesses to the liturgical nature of the creeds.

Chapter XIV

Let us briefly summarize what our many considerations have established. By an uncontestable argument we have made clear that the Holy Spirit exists from the Son just as He exists from the Father. He does not exist, however, as if from two different sources, but only from one; for He exists from that in virtue of which the Father and the Son are one, that is, from God, and not from that in virtue of which they are different from each other. But since God, from whom the Holy Spirit exists, is Father and Son, it is true to say that the Holy Spirit exists from the Father and from the Son, who are two. And since the Father does not exist earlier or later than the Son, and is not greater or lesser than the Son, and is not more or less God than the Son—therefore, the Holy Spirit does not exist from the Father before He exists from the Son, nor from the Son before He exists from the Father. Nor is His existing from the Father something greater or something lesser than His existing from the Son; nor does He exist more or less from the one than from the other. For if He were to exist earlier or later, or be greater or lesser, or be more or less from the one than from the other, then one or the other of these conclusions would have to follow: either (1) the Holy Spirit would not derive His existence from that in virtue of which the Father and the Son are one or (2) this unity would not be perfectly and simply one, but there would be some diversity implied in it, from which there would follow a diversity in the way the Holy Spirit existed from it. But it cannot be said that the Holy Spirit does not exist from that in virtue of which the Father and the Son are one, for then He would not be God. And it should not be believed that in the one God Himself there is according to His essence some diversity. Therefore, the Holy Spirit exists from the Father neither earlier nor later than from the Son; nor is the Holy Spirit either greater or lesser, or more or less from the Father than from the Son. For one and the same Holy Spirit, who exists wholly at once from the whole deity,

cannot exist more or less from the unity and consummate simplicity of God.

If it is said that the Holy Spirit exists principally[7] from the
Father—as if He existed more from the Father than from the
Son—then this ought not to be construed as involving any of the
differences mentioned above. But since the Son has that which
He is from the Father, it is not inconsistent to assert that the
existence of the Holy Spirit from the Son is also received by the
Son from the Father. Now, the Son's existence from the Father
is such that the Son is in every way that which the Father is, and
one and the same God with the Father. The God who is unique
and without composition cannot be greater or lesser than Himself, nor earlier nor later than Himself; nor can He have any
kind of diversity within Himself. Accordingly, therefore, the
Son is neither earlier nor later, nor greater nor lesser, than the
Father; nor does He have anything in Himself which is different
from the Father. So, since the Son exists perfectly from the
Father, He has perfect equality with Him and perfect likeness to
Him. Indeed, He has the same essence. Therefore, just as the
Father is not God more than the Son is God (even though the
Son exists from the Father), so the Holy Spirit does not exist
more from the Father than from the Son (even though the Son
exists from the Father in such a way that the Holy Spirit exists
from the Son). For, in so far as the Son is one and the same as
the Father, i.e., in so far as He is God, the Son is not one and the
Father another, nor does the Son have anything different—because the Father is not one God and the Son another God, nor
are they different in that which they are. But they are different
through that whereby the one is Father and the other is Son, i.e.,
through that whereby the Father is one person and the Son
another. And just as the Son is not a different God from the
Father, so, according to the fact that He is God, the Son has
nothing from anyone other than Himself. For when we say ''God
from God'' (meaning ''the Son from the Father'') we do not
understand one God to be existing from another God, but the

7. Cf. Augustine, Sermon 71 (PL, 38:459).

same God to be existing from the same God—even though we say "someone from someone else," i.e., Son from Father. For as has been said above, just as God, as called by a name which signifies unity, admits of no diversity, so, as called by names signifying God from God, He necessarily admits of plurality. If, therefore, it is said that the Holy Spirit exists principally from the Father, nothing else is signified than that the Son, from whom the Holy Spirit exists, exists from the Father in such a way that the Holy Spirit exists from the Son. For that which the Son is He has from the Father. There is no parallel here to created things, where, when we assert something to be "principally," we mean to signify that the thing which is said to be "principally" is greater than that with which it is compared. For example, when a steward, according to his master's command, attends to the feeding of a household, we rightly say that the master is "principally" and more the provider of the house than is the steward. For not everything which belongs to the master is equally the steward's; but that which is the Father's is also the Son's, and there is no inequality.

Perhaps someone will marvel and ask: "How can we understand that something exists from something else, so that the thing from which it exists is not of greater dignity and is not primary, and so that the thing which exists from the other is not less in some way and, hence, secondary? This appears especially to be the case since that which exists from another seems to be in need of that other for its existence—while the other seems in no way in need of that which exists from itself." To this we must reply as follows: just as the essence of God is quite different from created essence, so when we say that God exists from God by generation or procession, this generation or procession is to be understood quite differently from our speaking of things being born or proceeding from created things. For in God there is neither naturally nor temporally nor in any other sense anything either before or after, or greater or lesser; nor is there anything that can be rationally understood as a need. But everything that God is, is not so much equal or similar to God and coeternal with God as it is identical with God Himself. For

God is completely sufficient unto Himself, and there is nothing begotten and nothing proceeding from Him in the sense of something passing from not-being into being. Therefore, just as our intellect cannot reach beyond eternity to pass judgment on its own source, as it were, so we neither can nor ought to judge or understand God's generation or procession in terms of any likeness to creatures. But in God neither that which is born nor that which proceeds is different from that from which it is born or proceeds, namely, the one and only God. Therefore, just as the same God is not greater or lesser than Himself, so with respect to the three persons—viz., the Father, the Son, and the Holy Spirit—no person is more or less what He is than the other two; and this conclusion still holds true even though God exists from God by generation and by procession.

So we have seen with how much truth and necessity it follows that the Holy Spirit proceeds from the Son. But if this doctrine be false, then either something is false in those premises from which we have demonstrated this doctrine or else we have not argued correctly. But to assert that the premises are false is against the Christian faith which we and the Greeks affirm; and it cannot be shown that our argument is faulty. For this reason, if this doctrine of procession is not true, then the Christian faith is destroyed. And to one who understands, it is also clear that if the doctrine is asserted to be false, no truth follows from it.[8]

8. Anselm rightly sees that if a proposition (or a set of propositions) is true, then any other proposition validly deducible from it is also true. In the present passage he is not going on to suggest the general (and wrong) point that from false premises no true conclusion can validly follow. His method throughout *De Processione* has been to start with theological premises which both Latin and Greek churches agree to be essential to Christianity and from these premises to show that the *filioque* doctrine follows validly. Should the Greeks then continue to maintain that the *filioque* doctrine is false, they will be forced to assert the falsity of the premises from which the doctrine validly follows (assuming that it does follow validly). But since the Greeks cannot ascribe falsity to those premises without surrendering Christianity, they must, argues Anselm, concede the truth of the *filioque* doctrine. Thus, Anselm is saying, because Christianity is true, any denial of its truth is necessarily false. And rejection of the doctrine that the Holy Spirit proceeds also from the Son leads to this very falsehood. In this particular sense (rather than in a general sense) no truth follows from asserting that the *filioque* doctrine is false.

Now let us consider what happens when we assert that this doctrine is true. If it is true that the Holy Spirit proceeds from the Son just as He proceeds from the Father, then it follows that He is the Spirit of the Son as He is the Spirit of the Father, and that He is sent and given by the Son just as He is sent and given by the Father (which is what divine authority teaches); and absolutely no falsehood follows from the doctrine of procession. So, if the doctrine of procession from the Son be denied, then the premises from which the doctrine follows are false, the Christian faith is destroyed, and no truth is derivative from the doctrine; but if the doctrine of procession from the Son be affirmed, there follows such truth as we have discussed, with no falsity ensuing. Since these are the options, let the rational heart ask itself how this doctrine could reasonably be excluded from the Christian faith.

Finally, if it is an error to believe in this procession of the Holy Spirit from the Son, then divine authority itself leads us into error. For divine authority teaches us both those premises from which the doctrine of the procession from the Son follows and those implications which follow from this doctrine. And divine authority does not anywhere deny this procession from the Son, nor does it affirm anything which contradicts it in any way. If, therefore, the Greeks contend that this doctrine ought not to be taught because divine authority nowhere sets it forth, then let us counter by asserting that since Scripture nowhere denies this doctrine or says anything against it, the doctrine must not be denied. For we say that divine authority affirms this procession sufficiently when it affirms those things from whence procession can be proved, and when it in no way states anything whereby procession can be denied.

CHAPTER XV

So I have now made clear what I promised above. For the Son and the Holy Spirit cannot be given each other's name—not only because the Son exists by being begotten and the Holy Spirit by proceeding, but also because the Holy Spirit exists from the Son. But only the latter reason proves that the Son cannot be from the Holy Spirit. For we have seen that either the Son exists from the Holy Spirit or the Holy Spirit exists from the Son; and, hence, if the Holy Spirit did not exist from the Son, it would follow that the Son exists from the Holy Spirit.

So from our arguments above it is now clear that (1) the Father is God from whom God exists, but is not Himself God from God; (2) the Son is God from God, and God from whom God exists; and (3) the Holy Spirit is God from God, but not God from whom God exists. Although two exist from the Father —viz., the Son and the Holy Spirit—nevertheless, there are not two gods from the Father, but only one God, who is Son and Holy Spirit. And although there is one from whom the Son exists and another who exists from the Son—viz., the Father and the Holy Spirit—nevertheless, these are not two gods, but only one God, who is Father and Holy Spirit. And although the Holy Spirit exists from two—viz., from the Father and from the Son—nevertheless, it is not from two gods that He exists but from the one God, who is Father and Son.

Now, if Father and Son and Holy Spirit be considered two at a time, then it is clear from what has been said above that it is necessary for one of the two either to exist from the other because He does not exist from Himself or for that same one not to exist from the other because He does exist from Himself. Now, if we consider the Father and the Son, we see that the Son exists from the Father because the Father does not exist from the Son. And the Father does not exist from the Son because the Son exists from the Father. Similarly, if we consider the Father and the Holy Spirit, we see that the Holy Spirit exists from the Father because the Father does not exist from the Holy Spirit; and we see that the Father does not exist from the Holy Spirit because the Holy Spirit exists from the Father. So, also, if we ask ourselves how the Son and the Holy Spirit are related to each other, then we will see that the Holy Spirit exists from the Son because the Son does not exist from the Holy Spirit; and we will see that the Son does not exist from the Holy Spirit because the

Holy Spirit exists from the Son. Therefore, it is clear (as I have already said) that although these relations are present in one God, they cannot introduce their plurality into God's unity; nor can the unity of God introduce its singularity into these relations.

Chapter XVI

Now, there are six distinctions among the Father, the Son, and the Holy Spirit which grow out of these names: (1) to have a father, (2) not to have a father, (3) to have a son, (4) not to have a son, (5) to have a spirit proceeding from oneself, (6) not to have a spirit proceeding from oneself. Each of the persons has one property (from among these distinctions) by which He is different from the other two persons, and He has two common properties, so that by what He shares with one person He differs from the other. For the Father alone has a son, and in this respect He is different from the other two. Further, He has the Holy Spirit proceeding from Himself; and He has this property in common with the Son, and by it He is different from the Holy Spirit. Moreover, the Father does not have a father; and in this respect He is like the Holy Spirit and different from the Son. The Son alone has a father, and in this respect He is different from both the Father and the Holy Spirit. The Son shares with the Father the fact that the Holy Spirit proceeds from Him, and in this respect He is different from the Holy Spirit. Moreover, the Son is without a son just as the Holy Spirit is without a son, and in this the Son is different from the Father. The Holy Spirit alone is the one from whom no one proceeds. He holds the property of not having a father in common with the Father, and in this respect He is different from the Son. The Holy Spirit shares with the Son the property of not having a son, and so differs from the Father. So, then, it is the Father alone who exists from no one, and from Him the two others exist. It is the Holy Spirit alone who exists from two but from whom no one else exists. And it is the Son alone who exists from one and from whom one other exists. Moreover, it is common to the three persons that each one stands in relation to two others: for the Father is related to the Son and the Holy Spirit as to those who exist from Him. The Son is related to the Father and the Holy Spirit, since He is from the Father and the Holy Spirit is from the Son. And the Holy Spirit is related to the Father and the Son because He exists from both of them.

Therefore, each one possesses His own properties, the particular distribution of which is not the same in the other two. This is like the differences among human persons. For human persons are different from one another because the distribution of properties peculiar to one is not the same in the others. Nevertheless, this likeness is not perfect. For with regard to human persons, if there is one person, there is one man; and if there is one man, there is one person. Likewise, if there be several persons, there are also several men; and if there are several men, then their persons do not escape plurality. However, in God, although there are three persons, there is but one God. And, although there is but one God, the persons do not lose their plurality. So when we speak of the relation of God to God, we admit a diversity of persons which is like the diversity of persons which characterizes several men; but when we speak of God per se, i.e., of God in Himself, then He has an inseparable singularity which is like that of a single man. For a plurality of human persons does not exist except in several men, nor can one man admit a plurality of persons. But the one God is three persons and the three persons are one God. Hence, God does not fully possess the property of human persons—either with respect to their unity or with respect to their diversity.

I shall briefly discuss why the above point is true—although I have said a little about it in the preface of my epistle *On the Incarnation of the Word*. We often find that a plurality of things concur as one under a single name or under that same quantity which they had as individuals before they concurred as one. For example, if we put one point [i.e., one dot] on top of another with no space between, or if we draw one line upon another of an equal length, or if we lay upon one surface another which is equal to it, then we have but one point, one line, and one surface. And in many things like this, if one cares to observe it, the case is the same. So in this fashion there are not many eternities but only one eternity when we say "eternity within eternity." And when one light shines within another and we say "light within light," there is but one light. In the same way, whatever we say about the essence of God indicates neither an increase in quantity nor an admission of plurality even if it signifies a repetition in God. For, since God is eternity and since there is nothing at all beyond eternity, so beyond God there is nothing at all. And just as "eternity within eternity" indicates only one eternity, so "God within God" indicates only one God.

Now, we maintain out of true faith that God exists by generation from God and that God exists by procession from God. But because there is nothing beyond God, then when God is begotten from God or when God proceeds from God, the one who is begotten and the one who proceeds do not go out beyond God, but rather remain within God. Therefore, since God within God is only one God, then when God is begotten from God there is only one God—begetting and begotten. And when God proceeds from God, there is only one God—the one who proceeds and the one from whom He proceeds. So it follows inescapably that because God has no parts and is wholly whatever He is, that He is wholly Father and wholly Son and wholly Holy Spirit—and He is one and the same God, and not one God and another God. Therefore, in so far as Father, Son, and Holy Spirit are only one God (inasmuch as when God exists from God, God is within God), they retain in their deity the likeness to the singularity of an individual man. But in so far as God exists from God either by being begotten or by proceeding, then (since the one who is from someone cannot be that someone from whom he is) the relation of persons signified by the names "Father," "Son," and "Holy Spirit" resembles a plurality of persons.

Nevertheless, it ought to be observed that God does not exist apart from person, nor does person exist apart from God. It must also be noticed that sometimes we attribute to particular persons their own particular properties; and sometimes we attribute to someone, as if proper to him, that which is common to others. For when we say, "The Father is the only one of the three persons who derives existence from no one else; and the Son is the only one who exists from one and from whom another exists; and the Holy Spirit is the only one from whom no one exists"— then we attribute to each person His own property. But when we read, "No one knows the Son except the Father, or the Father except the Son" (Matt. 11:27) and "No one knows the things of God except the Spirit of God" (I Cor. 2:11), then although the Scriptures seem to deny to the other persons what it says concerning one, nevertheless what it attributes to one person as if peculiar to that person is common to them all. For neither the Father nor the Son is ignorant of Himself nor of the things that are God's; nor is the Holy Spirit ignorant of the Father or of the Son. And we have already sufficiently discussed why and when we should understand as referring to all three persons that which Scripture says about one person as if referring to Him alone.

In response to several pressing demands, I have presumed to write this treatise concerning the procession of the Holy Spirit and to defend the Latins against the arguments of the Greeks. In this endeavor I have not relied upon myself but only upon the Holy Spirit Himself. On this occasion I have presumed to add something about the unity of deity and the trinity of persons, although there are countless other men among those who write Latin who could have done this work better than I. Therefore, whatever I have said that seems worthy of acceptance, attribute it not to me but to the Spirit of Truth. And if there is something set forth which in any way needs correction, impute this to me but not to the understanding of the Latin Church.

Letters on
the Sacraments
Epistolae de Sacramentis

THE SACRIFICE OF LEAVENED AND UNLEAVENED BREAD
(*Epistola de Sacrificio Azimi et Fermentati*)

Anselm, servant of the Church of Canterbury, to Walram, Bishop of Naumburg.

To a knowledgeable man I speak briefly. If I were sure that Your Wisdom did not favor the successor of Julius Caesar and of Nero and of Julian the Apostate over the successor and Vicar of the Apostle Peter, most willingly would I greet you as "most beloved and reverend Bishop."[1] But since we must, to the best of our ability, fail no one in the defense of the true doctrine which you seek in order to argue against the Greeks who have come to you, I have sent you the tract *On the Procession of the Holy Spirit,* which I published against them.

I

Now, as to the sacrifice: what the Greeks think of it is different from what we hold; yet to many judicious Catholics the rite of the Greeks does not seem to be contrary to the Christian faith, for in both cases bread is consecrated, be it unleavened or

1. Anselm is here alluding to the investiture controversy which was raging in Germany. In this dispute Walram had at first sided against the papacy.

leavened. And when we read of the Lord, producing His Body from bread, that He "took bread and blessed it," unleavened or leavened is not specified (Matt. 26:26). It is certain, however, that it was unleavened bread that He blessed: not perhaps because what He was doing required it but because at the meal where this was done unleavened bread was accustomed to be served. Again, when elsewhere He called Himself and His Flesh "Bread"—because just as man sustains his temporal life by common bread, so by this Bread man lives forever—He does not say "unleavened" or "leavened," since it is equally bread in both cases. As a matter of fact, unleavened bread is not, as some believe, essentially different from leavened bread—any more than the new man before sin is essentially different from the man grown old in the leaven of sin. It seems, therefore, that the only reason for having called Himself and His Flesh "Bread," and for having produced His Body from bread, was to indicate that just as common bread, either unleavened or leavened, gives transitory life, so His Body gives eternal life. Whether the bread of His Body be leavened or unleavened is of no account. It is true that in the Law, where nearly everything bore a typal meaning, it is prescribed to eat unleavened bread during the feast of Passover. This was commanded in order to show that the Messiah whom the Jews were expecting was to be pure and innocent and in order to admonish us who were to eat of His Body that we too should be pure, free of all "leaven of malice and wickedness" (I Cor. 5:8). Now, however, that we have passed from ancient foreshadowing to new reality, now that we eat the unleavened Flesh of Christ, we have no need of this former symbolism in the bread from which we produce the Flesh itself.

II

It is quite evident, however, that it is better to consecrate unleavened bread than leavened bread—not only because it can be done much more suitably, more simply, more exactly, but also because that is what the Lord did. Hence, it is not to be passed over in silence that when the Greeks anathematize the "azimites"—that is the name they give us—they are anathematizing Christ Himself. Again, if they say that we judaize, then they must say that Christ also judaized. And if they claim that Christ produced His Eucharistic Body from unleavened bread in order to observe the Judaistic precept about unleavened bread, then they fall into an egregious error, since they believe that He infected the pure newness with the leaven of obsolescence. It is evident, therefore, that when Christ used unleavened bread for the institution of the Eucharist, He did not do so in order to observe the precept about unleavened bread. Rather, He did so either to approve the "azimites" while reproving the "fermentarians," whose existence He foresaw, or else so that if the "fermentarians" were approved, He would be approving the "azimites" also.

III

It is not true, as they say, that we judaize: we do consecrate unleavened bread—not, however, to observe the Old Law but rather to perform the rite more diligently, and also to imitate the Lord, who certainly performed it without judaizing. When we do something which the Jews did to observe Judaism, we do not thereby judaize, as long as we are acting not for the sake of Judaism but for some other reason. If, for instance, during the days of Passover one eats unleavened bread—either because he has no other kind or simply because he prefers unleavened to leavened bread—or if one must submit to circumcision for reasons of health, or again if a man does not muzzle his threshing ox lest it go hungry: only a fool will conclude that by doing these things one is judaizing. When, therefore, we consecrate unleavened bread, we attach to its use no symbolic meaning with reference to the Lord Jesus, who is to come. Rather, just as He Himself did, we consecrate the bread so that by divine power it may be changed into His Body. In doing this we are in no way observing the Old Law but rendering honor to the truth of the Gospel.

Finally, when He Himself performed this same rite, He said to

His disciples, "Do this for a commemoration of me" (Luke 22:19). Now, if He had not wanted us (for in giving this command to His disciples He was also giving it to us) to consecrate unleavened bread, He should have forewarned us (by forewarning His disciples) and said, Do not do it with unleavened bread. Since, therefore, by saying simply "Do this" He did not exclude unleavened bread, who is the man whose wisdom dares to rule out what the Lord Himself did, or to prohibit what He Himself not only did not prohibit by word, but even prescribed by His action? Who, I say, but one "more wise than it behoveth to be wise" is so sure of his own wisdom as to boldly make the following claim: "We understand the Lord's words 'Do this,' to mean 'Do what I am doing.' But we do not understand the words to mean 'Do what I am doing with that which I am doing it.' " Moreover, in performing divine actions we ought to use what we deem to be more worthy. Now, since it is clear that the sacrifice in question must be celebrated with the substance of bread, either unleavened or leavened, what kind of bread will be deemed the more worthy to be used in producing the reality of the Lord's Body if not that bread chosen by both the Old Law and the Gospel (for the Old Law foreshadows the same reality which the Gospel manifests)? If, then, our answer to the Greeks is that we consecrate unleavened bread not because of any figurative sense but because of the above-mentioned reasons, it is impossible to understand why the Greeks think they may rightly regard us as deserving of anathema or at least censure.

IV

Now, if they say that we cannot consecrate with unleavened bread without including the figurative sense (and this would be a proof that we are judaizing), we conclude that, in like manner, neither can they use leavened bread in the consecration without including the figurative meaning, because by leaven both the Old Testament and the New signify sin: the Old, when it curses the eating of leavened bread during Passover and the New when it

warns us to feast on our Passover "not with the old leaven, nor
with the leaven of malice and wickedness" (I Cor. 5:8). We say
that we do not judaize even if we admit a figurative sense in "unleavened bread," because we do not thereby signify, as the Jews
do, that Christ is to come free from the leaven of sin; but as
Christians we show that this Christ, free from sin, has already
come. And by this use of unleavened bread we are admonished to
appear and really be like the Passover of unleavened bread that
we eat. But in this matter our opponents profess themselves
neither Jews nor Christians, because by the use of leaven they
signify neither that God is to come without sin, as do the Jews,
nor that He has already so come, as do the Christians. They seem
rather to favor the heathen, who consider Him as leavened by sin
like other men.

If, now, they say that Christians should not make use of
figures or types because "the old things" (in which figures were
necessary) "are passed away" (II Cor. 5:17), then let them
deny—not to mention other things—that baptism is the type of a
particular death and burial, thus contradicting the Apostle, who
says: "All who are baptized in Christ Jesus are baptized into
His death. For we are buried together with Him by baptism into
death" (Rom. 6:3–4). Or if they allow us to use types, but not
those used in the Old Law (and therefore unleavened bread is
not to be used to convey a figurative meaning, since it was used
for that purpose in the Old Law), then let them not baptize in
water, because "our fathers all in Moses were baptized in the
cloud and in the sea" (I Cor. 10:1). Now, this expression un-
deniably had a figurative meaning. Moreover, let them not
baptize in water lest they appear to baptize with the baptism of
John, who baptized in water. If, therefore, in baptizing in water,
which has a figurative sense, we are blameless, despite the fact
that the old baptism, which was a type of the new one, was also
done with water, then what is this great wisdom of the Greeks?
With what wisdom do the Greeks curse us for using unleavened
bread in the sacrifice of the Body of Christ, who is our Passover?
For the old Passover, the type of our own, was also celebrated
with unleavened bread. By this symbol we either commemorate

the fact that He whose Body we sacrifice was unleavened (i.e.,
free from any corruption of sin) or else we admonish ourselves,
who partake of His Body, that we must be unleavened. Thus the
Apostle says: "Purge out the old leaven, that you may be a new
dough, as you are unleavened. For Christ our Passover is sacrificed. Therefore let us feast, not with the old leaven, nor with the
leaven of malice and wickedness, but with the unleavened bread
of sincerity and truth" (I Cor. 5:7-8).

V

Therefore, whether or not we intend any figurative meaning
in our use of unleavened bread in the sacrifice, the Greeks can in
no way prove us reprehensible; rather, in the offering of the
sacrifice, either we alone do rightly and they do not, or if they do
rightly, then we do better and more correctly. Indeed, they show
plainly enough that they have no reason in support of their
position and against ours, since what they present against us is
known to militate in no way against us nor in their favor. As I
have read in your letter, they quote as objections against us the
words of the Apostle: "For the letter killeth, but the spirit
quickeneth" (II Cor. 3:6), and the words of the prophet Amos:
"Offer a sacrifice of praise with leaven" (Amos 4:5). And so
they try to show that "the letter" prescribing the use of unleavened bread in the celebration of the old Passover "kills" us,
since we are observing it by using unleavened bread in our
sacrifice; but they do not rightly understand the words of the
Apostle. For, according to him, "the letter kills" when by
forbidding sin it reveals it, because, without the help of grace to
do what is commanded, it makes man disobedient and sinful. The
same Apostle sets this forth quite clearly in the epistle to the
Romans by these words: "I did not know sin by the Law. For I
had not known concupiscence, if the Law did not say: Thou shalt
not covet. But sin taking occasion by the commandment wrought
in me all manner of concupiscence. For without the Law sin was
dead, and I lived some time without the Law. But when the
commandment came, sin revived. And I died, and the command-

ment that was ordained to life, the same was found to be unto death to me. For sin taking occasion by the commandment seduced me, and by it killed me" (Rom. 7:7–11). So, then, "the letter" without the help of grace "killeth." "But the spirit quickeneth," as the same Apostle says to Titus: "But when the goodness and kindness of God our Savior appeared, not by the works of justice, which we have done, but according to His mercy He saved us by the laver (washing) of regeneration and the renewing of the Holy Spirit, whom He hath poured forth upon us abundantly through Jesus Christ our Savior, that being justified by His grace, we may be heirs, according to hope of life everlasting" (Titus 3:4–7). When, therefore, he had said, "Our sufficiency is from God, who also hath made us fit ministers of the New Testament [Covenant], not in the letter, but in the Spirit," he added, "For the letter killeth, but the spirit quickeneth" (II Cor. 3:5–6). As if to say: God made us "ministers of the New Testament [Covenant]," which is not in a letter that kills, as was the Old Covenant, but in a life-giving spirit. And to both the letter that kills and the Spirit that gives life, applies what he adds further:

Now if the ministration of death, engraven with letters upon stones, was glorious—so that the children of Israel could not steadfastly behold the face of Moses, because of the glory of his countenance, a glory done away with—how shall not the ministration of the Spirit be more glorious? For if the ministration of condemnation be glory, much more the ministration of justice aboundeth in glory. For even that which is glorious [i.e., the former ministration] was in this respect not really glorified, because of the glory [of the latter ministration] that excelleth. For if that which is transient was glorious, much more that which remaineth is in glory. Having therefore such hopes, we show much confidence, and are not like Moses, who put a veil upon his face so that the children of Israel might not steadfastly look on his countenance. Now this glory is done away with; and the senses of the Israelites were made dull. For until this present day, the very same veil, in the reading of the Old Testament, remaineth not taken away, because in Christ it is made void. But even until this day, when Moses is read, the veil is upon their heart. But when one shall turn to the Lord, the veil shall be taken away. Now the Lord is a spirit; and where the Spirit of God is, there is liberty. But we all beholding the glory of the Lord with open face are transformed into the same image from glory to glory, as by the Spirit of the Lord. Therefore seeing that we have this ministration, according as we have obtained mercy, we faint not (II Cor. 3:7–4:1).

It seems superfluous to add anything to this concerning the killing by the letter and the life-giving by the Spirit. It is therefore clear that what the Greeks object to about this letter that kills is neither in their favor nor against our position.

VI

Now, as to what the Greeks quote from the prophet: "Come to Gilgal and do wickedly" and "offer a sacrifice of praise with leaven" (Amos 4:4–5). These words of the prophet are to be understood either as approving such a sacrifice or as reproving it. Now, if the prophet prescribes and approves this—I am speaking as they do—then this "letter kills" them, since they observe this letter by sacrificing with leavened bread. But if this is said by way of reproof, then how great is their impudence in using in their sacrifices what the prophet execrates in a sacrifice. And on what grounds do they quote those words as an authority in their favor? There is no doubt, however, that the prophet here did not prescribe; but rather he reproved, since he associated this sacrifice with a wicked action. For he said: "Come to Bethel and do wickedly." And shortly after, continuing his condemnation, he says: "And offer a sacrifice of praise with leaven." Therefore, let the "fermentarians" either present as strong a reason in defending their position as do the "azimites" in strengthening theirs; or let them cast away their leaven and become "azimites"; or if they cannot do the former nor consent to do the latter, let them at least not find fault with the "azimites."

VII

In the third question—as I understand it—you have written that the Greeks denounce our marriages in which blood-related persons [i.e., persons belonging to one blood-related group] are

joined to blood-related persons from another blood-related group.
I see no authority nor reason for their view. For, if on their part
they forbid this in their marriages, either they do not extend the
relationships to the seventh generation, as we do, or else what
they prescribe seems to be impossible to observe. Since there are
often in one related group more than a hundred men and women
wanting to marry, it is then necessary to find that many [i.e.,
one hundred] related groups from each of which to choose only
one person for each man and each woman of that one first group
to marry. Either, therefore, their own marriages are unquestion-
ably condemnable if they are entered into within seven genera-
tions (and they should not reprove ours in which blood relatives
are united to blood relatives from another group—which is
forbidden by no authority or reason) or it is impossible, as I
have said, to observe what they prescribe—that is, to seek out as
many related groups for the marriages of one group as there are
in this group men and women requesting marriage. Now, that
which is done against reason and without any authority is
without a doubt reasonably repudiated.

Bishop Walram to Anselm
(*Epistola Waleramni ad Anselmum*)

To the most serene Lord Anselm, most reverend archbishop of
Canterbury: Walram, bishop of Naumburg by the grace of God,
offers a servant's homage, constant prayers, and himself—most
devoted in all things.

It is most foolish to dare lay any claim to literary learning in
dealing with Minerva; and among eminent scholars it is not
within my power to reason convincingly by the force of my
arguments. But sighing with the prophet "Open Thou my eyes
and I will consider the wondrous things of Thy law" (Ps.
119:18), with supreme devotion I lift up my eyes to the mountain of Your Highness, so that from thence help may come to me.
Your help is "help from the Lord, who made heaven and earth"
(Ps. 121:2). "He who is joined to the Lord is one spirit" (I Cor.

6 :17), so that it is clear that from His fullness you search out
the deep things of God; while in our meanness we hear His voice,
but we are utterly ignorant of "whence He cometh or whither
He goeth" (John 3 :8).

I

God is undivided Trinity, and all who are in God are one in
Him. Now, diversity in the Church is directly opposed to unity.
And that which proceeds against itself by dissension among its
parts cannot stand for long. But Palestine believes one thing
about the sacraments of the Church, Armenia another, and our
Rome and three-part Gaul still another. Even the mystery of the
Lord's Body is performed one way in Rome, another way in
Gaul, and still more differently in our Germany. We have received from the ancient Fathers the rite of the sacrifice, and I
wonder greatly as to whence this novelty could have crept into
the house of God. "Jesus Christ yesterday and today, the same is
forever," always one, always the same, suffering no change
(Heb. 13 :8). He dissents from Christ who tends toward diversity. Christ is the Bread of angels, who came down from
Heaven and was made the Bread of men, the food of the poor,
the fullness of those who reign with Him : so that they who
worthily partake of Him live forever and ever. "We, being
many, are one bread, one body in Christ"—we who partake of
one bread (I Cor. 10 :17). Christ is the way on which we should
walk, He whom we should imitate. He who wanders away from
Christ walks in peril. While sacrificing, then, let us do what
Christ did, for He has said, "This do as often as you partake of
it" (I Cor. 11 :25).

II

The Armenians, for example, believe that with *leavened* bread
they are offering a sacrifice of praise. But they do not walk with
Christ "in newness of life" (Rom. 6 :4). True imitators of
Christ must feast "not with the old leaven" but with "the
unleavened bread of sincerity and truth" (I Cor. 5 :8). Even "a

little leaven corrupteth the whole lump" (I Cor. 5:6). Let not the incorruptible Body of Christ, in so far as is possible, be infected with any corruption. Let all such corruption be absent from the sacrifice of purity. And let those who long to put on the incorruption of Christ's Body strip themselves of the old man by means of the purity of the new sacrifice. In producing the Body of Christ it is unacceptable to use any substance other than that which He Himself offered. And, if I dare say so, the rule which He gave for sacrificing must be kept.

III

We bless the bread separately and the chalice separately. The canons and the ancient Roman Ordo prescribe this—namely, that from the beginning, in the canon, we trace a particular cross over each. We hold this as a public and time-honored custom everywhere, "from generation unto generation" (Luke 1:50), and we are amazed at your diversity. Christ did this and commanded us to do it. "Do this," He said, "as often as you partake of it" (I Cor. 11:25). Taking bread, He blessed it separately, and in like manner the chalice. He made a separate sign of the cross over each, as our Ordo and even the Roman Ordo prescribe. And thus our custom grew up from Him who is the same "yesterday and today and forever" (Heb. 13:8). On the matter of individual signs of the cross we are approved by the authority of Christ. So I greatly wonder how the diversity in sacrificing came about. There is "one faith, one baptism," one friend, spouse, and dove of Christ (Eph. 4:5). It is greatly harmful to the unity of the Church to differ in the matter of the sacraments, and to allow whatever one pleases.

IV

Furthermore, several while consecrating cover the chalice from the beginning; some do so with a corporal, others with a folded cloth, according to the likeness of the shroud which, we read, was found in the sepulcher, "not lying with the linen clothes, but apart, wrapped up into one place" (John 20:7). Now, Christ is

"the way and the truth and the life" (John 14:6). He is the way
on which we must walk so that we may come to Him. "He that
saith he abideth in Christ ought himself also to walk even as He
walked" (I John 2:6). None but the true imitators of the Life
come to the Life. The paschal Victim was immolated uncovered
in body on the altar of the cross. He willed to be offered uncovered in body, who unveiled to His own all that He heard from
His Father. In His immolation He revealed Himself "as He is"
(I John 3:2); and we shall behold His glory "with open face,"
so as to be conformed to Him in all things and be "made like to
the Body of His glory" so that He Himself may be all to us in
eternal bliss (II Cor. 3:18; Phil. 3:21; I Cor. 15:28). And to use
His own words, "It is finished" (John 19:30). He said this so
that we may not doubt that the old things have passed away and
that all things are new (II Cor. 5:17). The veil of the temple was
rent from the top even to the bottom. And even until this day a
veil is upon the hearts of the Jews, so that though having eyes
they do not see and having ears they do not understand. We,
however, to whom God hath revealed these things by His Spirit
ought not to confound the mysteries of sacrificing; but, following the example of the Lord Jesus, we ought to make them clear.
Let us not, with Moses, place over them the veil of the Jews; but
offering with the Lord Jesus, let us strive to be brought over
from glory to glory. Let Jesus, who was naked on the altar of the
cross, appear naked on the altar of our immolation. That which
we proclaim in words, let us carry out by deeds. That bread is
truly the Body of Christ: it should also be sacrificed as the
immolation of the Body of Christ. The Body of Christ, uncovered on the altar of the cross, was wrapped up in linens in the
sepulcher. Naked in His passion, He was wrapped up in His
burial, through the devotion of His disciples. Burying Him
according to the custom of the Jews, they showed their zealous
devotion to their Master; but they were still ignorant of the
truth of the sacrament. They buried Him as a Jew who re-
sembled the Jews, because they had not yet carefully pondered
the mystery of the cross. "The Spirit searcheth all things, yea,

even the deep things of God'' (I Cor. 2:10). But the Spirit had
not yet been given to them because Jesus, crucified in His
weakness, had not yet been glorified. But, once glorified, He put
away the clothes of corruption, He took off corruptible things,
having put on incorruption; He left the sepulcher, He mani-
fested His glory to those who loved Him. Why, then, do we, by
wrapping Him in a corruptible shroud, proclaim, as it were, the
weakness of Christ and His concealment in darkness when most
truly we proclaim Him as the power of God and the light of the
world? Let not the ''light of light, which enlighteneth every
man'' in any way be put under the bushel of a shroud (John
8:12). But as He Himself, Priest and Victim, offered Himself, so
let our sacrifice be offered to Him. Placed under the open sky, let
it shine for all unto life in the house of Christ. Then will our
Victim be most acceptable, if it be similar to Christ's Victim.
However, we also enwrap the life-giving Victim not from the
beginning, as is your custom, but at the end, with Joseph and
Nicodemus. That which is offered not only in appearance, but
also in the truth of the thing, ought not to differ in its immolation. He who differs does not himself also walk even as Christ
walked (I John 2:6). And if on this score the purity of the
sacrifice is provided for, it is most easy with us to safeguard
cleanliness under the cover of purity, without deviating at the
very beginning from a most ancient rite of the Church.

V

Let your ''eyes see my imperfect being'' (Ps. 139:16); and
since you are filled as by the hands of the virtues, with the whole
fullness of prudential knowledge, may you have compassion on
our extreme imperfection. The Catholic Church glorifies God in
me because the grace of divine goodness is apparent in our
conversion. ''By the grace of God I am what I am'' (I Cor.
15:10). From Saul I have become Paul; from an enemy of the
Catholic Church I have become an intimate friend, in highest
favor with Pope Paschal, sharing the secrets of the cardinals. On
that account I am hopeful of prosperous success in all things.

Like Joseph in the house of Pharaoh, so am I in the palace of Emperor Henry,[2] "Neither is it my iniquity nor my sin" (Ps. 59:3) if, which God forbid, I am either as Nero the incestuous or as Julian the Apostate. Thanks be to God because under the rule of Your Holiness, the wolf and the lamb pasture together, the lion and the calf lie down together, and a little child leads them. And because "the scepter of Your kingdom is a scepter of uprightness" (Heb. 1:8), we praise the strength of God because the wild beasts have become tame in the fear of the Church and harm no one on the mount of the Lord's powers. "The lion shall roar; who will not fear?" (Amos 3:8). But because the just man is bold as a lion (Prov. 28:1), your heart, like that of strong-handed David himself, does not fear in such things, but triumphs in all things by the power of God. God, who has anointed you "with the oil of gladness above your fellows" (Heb. 1:9), will crown you "with mercy and compassion" (Ps. 103:4) in the kingdom of blessedness.

THE SACRAMENTS OF THE CHURCH
(Epistola de Sacramentis Ecclesiae)

To my Lord and friend Walram, venerable bishop of Naumburg by the grace of God, from Anselm, servant of the church of Canterbury: greeting, reverence, prayers, and the affection of love.

I rejoice and thank God because, as you have written, the Catholic Church glorifies Him in you; for in your promotion appears the grace of divine goodness. And I rejoice because you enjoy friendship and close acquaintance with the Lord Pope Paschal, while still allowing me to greet Your Holiness as a friend.

In your noble humility you compare me to Minerva and call me "Mountain." But I do not apply this to myself, for I perceive in me nothing worthy of these compliments. I must not,

---

2. Henry V, who reigned from 1106 to 1125.

however, be ungrateful to Your Benevolence, for you are doing it
out of the abundance of your good will toward me. For we are
wont often to think more highly of those we love than they
deserve. So my heart does not take pride in this praise, which
does not apply to me, but I gratefully rejoice in your love, which
is always dear to me.

I

Your Reverence asks about the Sacraments of the Church,
because they are not everywhere performed the same way but are
dealt with differently in different places. Indeed if they were
celebrated in one way and with one mind in the whole Church, it
would be good and praiseworthy. But there are many diversities
which do not conflict with the substance of the sacrament nor
with its efficacy nor with faith in it. And it is not possible to
bring all together into one practice. Accordingly, I think that
these diverse practices should rather be peacefully tolerated in
union of hearts than be scandalously condemned with discord.
For we have it from the holy Fathers that, provided the unity of
charity in the Catholic faith is preserved, a different practice
does no harm. But if one asks whence these diverse customs arise,
I can conceive of no place other than from the diversity of
human dispositions. Even though men do not disagree concerning the virtue and the truth of the thing, they do not agree on
the aptness and suitability of the manner of administration; for
what one deems more suitable, another often considers less
suitable. Nor do I believe that to disagree concerning these
diversities is to wander away from the truth of the thing itself.

II

In offering the sacrifice of the Body and Blood of the Lord,
some make one sign of the cross over each during the canon from
the beginning, while others make one sign over each only when
the bread or body is named individually and when the chalice or
blood is named individually. But these latter make only one sign
over both when the offering, or the Victim, is named—because as

Christ is one, who offered Himself for us, so the offering is one and the Victim which we offer in the bread and wine is one. I do not see that in doing this these last dissent more from Christ, who blessed each individually, than all those dissent who do not consecrate the chalice after the supper, as Christ did, and who do not always do it in the evening, as Christ did, and who call both together by one name—"offering or Victim"—which Christ did not do. From this we may conclude that in such an action, provided we preserve the truth of the thing, we may differ from one another without blame, since we differ from the very Author of the sacrifice itself without offense.

Now, when we say "these gifts, these offerings, these holy sacrifices"—whether separate signs of the cross are made individually over the bread and over the wine, or whether both are consecrated together by one sign of the cross—I do not see in this diversity any reprehensible dissension, save that perhaps it is more fitting to sign both with one cross, as both are sanctified with one word of blessing. For when we bless several men or diverse things collectively, we do not impart to each a particular sign of the cross, but we believe that a single sign of the cross suffices for all.

III

Some cover the chalice from the beginning—some with a corporal, others with a folded cloth—to keep it clean. They do not leave the chalice bare, as Christ was crucified naked to show Himself symbolically revealed to the world. I do not see that they should be reproved on account of the nudity of Christ which they do not signify while sacrificing, any more than because they do not show in the same sacrifice that He was crucified outside the city, outside a house, and under the open sky. Yet these things are not devoid of meaning. For "Christ who suffered for us, leaving us an example so that we may follow in His footsteps" (I Pet. 2:21), also gave us in these things the example of enduring incomparable contempt and poverty for the sake of justice. In fact, He was considered so contemptible and judged so execrable that He was not deemed worthy to die inside any dwelling of men, nor among any men except the execrable, nor under any roof except the sky, from beneath which He could not be driven away. Thus, according to the prophet, He was regarded as "the scorn of men and the rejected of the people" (Ps. 22:6). Moreover, He was so poor that when He came into the world He was born not in His own but in another's house; and once born, He was placed, for want of room, in the manger of brute animals; and living in the world He had no place to rest His head; nor dying, anything to cover His nakedness; nor dead, anything to shroud Him; nor a sepulcher or a place where His dead body could be reposited.

One should rather imitate all these things in one's life by deeds, as reason demands, than signify the nakedness of Christ by the nudity of the sacrifice. Nor can I imagine why one should see to it that the sacrifice not be covered because Christ suffered naked, any more than that it not be performed under a roof or within a city because Christ suffered under the open sky outside the city. But if it is not the custom to offer it out from under a roof on account of the disturbances of the weather, there seems to be a similar reason for not uncovering the chalice during the sacrifice for fear of certain inconveniences which may happen. Therefore, I consider it safer and more diligent to cover the chalice—lest a fly or something undesirable fall into it, which to our knowledge often happens—than to expose it uncovered to possible impurities.

These things I answer to Your Wisdom according to my way of thinking, rejecting no one's better reason. About those who sacrifice with leavened bread I have erstwhile sent you a letter.

On the Harmony of the Foreknowledge, the Predestination, and the Grace of God with Free Choice

(De Concordia Praescientiae et Praedestinationis et Gratiae Dei cum Libero Arbitrio)

With the help of God I shall try to set forth in writing what He deigns to reveal to me concerning the three questions in which free choice seems to be incompatible with the foreknowledge, the predestination, and the grace of God.

Question One:
Concerning Foreknowledge and Free Choice

Chapter I

The foreknowledge of God seems to be incompatible with free choice; for the things foreknown by God will necessarily occur, whereas things which happen through free choice take place out of no necessity. But if these are incompatible, then it is impossible that there should also be an event which is brought about through freedom of choice. If, on the other hand, one perceives that there is no such impossibility, then the incompatibility which seems to hold is completely eliminated.

Therefore, let us posit both the foreknowledge of God, from which the necessity of future things seems to follow, and also freedom of choice, by which many things are believed to occur without any necessity; and let us see whether it is impossible for the two to coexist. If it is impossible, then there will arise a further impossibility, since an impossible thing is one which, if posited, is followed by another impossible thing. But assuming that there is some event which is going to happen without necessity, God foreknows it, for He foreknows every future event. But what God foreknows will necessarily occur in the same manner as He foreknows it to occur. It follows, then, that it is necessary that some event will occur without necessity. Therefore, it is true that what God foreknows will necessarily occur, but also true that God foreknows that an event will occur without any necessity. Consequently, to one who understands correctly, the foreknowledge from which necessity follows does not seem at all incompatible with freedom of choice, from which necessity is excluded.

But you will say to me: "Your reasoning does not do away with the necessity of my sinning or of my not sinning, because God foreknows whether I am going to sin or not sin; and therefore, if I sin, it is necessary for me to sin, and if I do not sin, it is necessary that I do not sin." To this I reply: You ought not to say merely "God foreknows that I am going to sin" or "God foreknows that I am not going to sin." But you should say "God foreknows that it is without necessity that I am going to sin" or "God foreknows that it is without necessity that I am not going to sin." From this latter formulation it follows that whether you sin or whether you do not sin, it will not be by necessity, because God foreknows that whichever you are to do shall be done without necessity. Do you see now that it is not impossible for the foreknowledge of God (according to which we say that things foreknown by God are going to occur by necessity) to coexist with freedom of choice (according to which many things are done without necessity)? For if this is impossible, then something impossible must follow. But no impossibility arises from this.

Perhaps you are thinking: "When you say that because of God's foreknowledge it is necessary that I am going either to sin or not to sin without necessity, you still have not shown that my heart is free from the influence of necessity. For necessity seems to have the ring of coercion or restraint. And, therefore, if it is necessary for me to sin willingly, I understand this to mean that some hidden force compels me to will to sin; and if I do not sin, I think it is because I am restrained by this force from willing to sin. For this reason it seems to me that if I sin I sin by necessity, and if I do not sin it is by necessity that I do not sin."

Chapter II

And I reply: We should realize that we often say it is necessary for something to occur even though there is nothing compelling it to occur, and that it is necessary for something not to occur even though there is nothing precluding it from occurring. We say, for instance, that it is necessary for God to be immortal and that it is necessary for God not to be unjust. But we do not mean that some power compels Him to be immortal or prevents Him from being unjust, because no power can prevent Him from being immortal or can compel Him to be unjust.[1] Similarly, I say it is necessary that you are going to sin or not going to sin by your will alone—in accordance with God's foreknowledge. But this must not be understood to mean that something prevents your act of will, which is not going to occur, or that something compels your act of will, which is going to occur. For God, who foresees what you are willingly going to do, foreknows that your will is not compelled or prevented by anything else; hence this activity of the will is free. If these things are carefully considered, I think it will be seen that no contradiction prevents

1. Cf. CDH, II, 17.

us from affirming both the foreknowledge of God and freedom of choice.

Finally, if one considers the proper meaning of the word "foreknow," he will see that when something is said to be foreknown, it is thus declared to be something that actually will occur. For, since knowledge can be only of what is the case, one can foreknow only what is going to happen. Therefore, when I say, "If God foreknows something, it is necessary that it be going to occur," this is the same as saying, "If something will occur, then necessarily it will occur." But this necessity neither compels a thing to be nor prevents it from being. And so by the very fact that something exists it is said necessarily to exist; and by the very fact that something does not exist it is said necessarily not to exist. In saying this we do not mean that some necessity is either compelling this thing to exist or not to exist, or preventing it from existing or not existing. For when I say, "If a thing will be, then necessarily it will be," this necessity follows, rather than precedes, the presumed existence of the thing.[2] The same thing would be true if I were to declare, "What will be, necessarily will be." For this necessity signifies nothing more than the impossibility that something will both be and not be at the same time.

Likewise, it can be true both that a thing's existence—past, present, or future—does not occur by necessity, and also that there is the necessity of its having been what it was or its being what it is or its going to be what it will be. Indeed, for a thing to be past is not the same as for a past thing to be past; nor is it the same thing for something to be present and for a present thing to be present, or for something to be future and for a future thing to be future—just as it is not the same for a thing to be white and for a white thing to be white. A piece of wood, for instance, is not necessarily white at all times; for at some time before it became white it was possible for it not to become white, and after it has become white it is possible for it to become not-white. But a white piece of wood is necessarily white at all times, because

2. On the distinction between antecedent and subsequent necessity, see CDH, II, 17.

neither before it existed nor after it existed as white is it possible for something white to be not-white at the same time. In the same way, a thing may be existing in the present without necessity—since before it began to exist in the present it was possible for it not to exist, and while it exists it is possible for it to cease existing in the present. But it is necessary for a present thing always to exist in the present—because neither before it existed nor after it is present is it possible for a present thing to be not-present at the same time.

In the same manner there may be something—a certain action, let us say—that is going to occur without necessity, because before it occurs it is possible for it not to occur. But it is necessary that what is going to happen be going to happen, since what is going to happen cannot be not going to happen. As regards the past, it is true that a thing may have happened without necessity, since before it occurred it was possible for it not to occur. But, likewise, it is always necessary that what has happened has happened, since it is impossible that what has happened has not happened. Now, the past event has a characteristic which neither the present nor the future event has. For what is past can never become not-past as what is present can become not-present and as what is going to occur without necessity can be not going to occur. And so when we say of what is going to occur that it is going to occur, this statement, like all other such statements whereby we predicate a thing of itself, must be true—because what is going to happen cannot be not going to happen. So too, "Every man is a man," "If he is a man he is a man," "Every white thing is white," and "If it is a white thing it is white" are necessarily true statements because something cannot both be and not be at the same time. Certainly, if it is not necessary that everything which is going to be *is* going to be, then something which is going to happen is not going to happen—a self-contradiction. Necessarily, therefore, everything which is going to happen is going to happen; and if it is going to happen, then it is going to happen—since [in these statements] the future thing is predicated of itself. But the necessity here is subsequent necessity, which does not compel anything to be.

Chapter III

However, a thing which we realize is going to happen need not in every case happen by necessity, although it is going to happen; for if I assert, "Tomorrow there is going to be a revolt in the country," it does not follow that the revolt will occur by necessity. For before it occurs it is possible for it not to occur, even though it will actually occur. Nonetheless, sometimes when we say that an event will occur, it is true that it will occur by necessity. An example of this is my stating "The sun is going to rise tomorrow." Therefore, if I state that a future thing is necessarily going to occur, this may be understood in two ways: (1) in the way that tomorrow's revolt is necessarily going to occur or (2) in the way that tomorrow's sunrise is necessarily going to occur. For the revolt, which is not necessitated, is called necessary solely on the basis of subsequent necessity—since we are saying about what is going to occur that it is going to occur. For if tomorrow there is to be a revolt, then, necessarily, tomorrow there is to be a revolt. Tomorrow's sunrise, however, is understood to be something that will occur by both kinds of necessity, namely, by antecedent necessity, which causes the event to occur (according to which the event will occur because it is necessary that it occur) and by subsequent necessity, which does not compel anything to occur (but according to which a thing that is to occur, necessarily is to occur).

Therefore, when we say of the events which God knows will occur, that it is necessary for them to occur, we do not always mean that something is going to occur by necessity—but rather that something which is going to occur, necessarily is going to occur; for what is indeed going to occur cannot at the same time be something that will not occur. We mean the same thing when we say simply "God foreknows such-and-such an event" without adding, "and this event is going to occur." For to foreknow something implies that that thing is going to happen. Indeed, "to foreknow" means nothing other than to know what is going to occur. And so, if God foreknows something, then it is necessary that the thing occur. Therefore, it does not follow from the foreknowledge of God that the thing foreknown will in every case occur by necessity. For, although He foreknows all future events, nevertheless He does not foreknow every future event as occurring by necessity. He foreknows that some things are going to occur through the free will of rational creatures.

We must note too that just as it is not necessary for God to will what He does, so in many cases it is not necessary for man to will what he does. And just as it is necessary that whatever God wills, should occur; so also in the things which God places under the control of the human will, it is necessary that what man wills, should occur. Accordingly, in such cases, if a man wills something it occurs; and if he does not will it, it does not occur. For it is impossible that what God wills should fail to occur. So when He wills that the will of man be neither compelled to will nor prevented from willing by any necessity, then it is necessary that man's will be free. And when God wills that the effect follow from the human will, it is necessary that what man wills, should occur. Accordingly, although a man does not by necessity will sin, nevertheless when he does will to sin, a sinful act necessarily occurs. If one were to ask whether a sin committed by the will through its willing occurs necessarily, the answer must be that just as the will does not will necessarily, neither does the sin of the will occur necessarily. Nor does the will commit sin necessarily, because if it did not will freely it would not act—even though, as I said above, what it does will, necessarily occurs. Now, to sin in this case is nothing other than to will what one ought not to will; so the sin of the will is not necessary, any more than willing a particular thing is necessary. But it is still true that if a man wills to sin, it is necessary that he sin; but he does so by that necessity which, as I have explained above, does not compel or prevent anything.

Thus the free will chooses something which it (1) is able to keep from willing and (2) is not able to keep from willing and (3) is necessary for it to will. For before it has willed, it is able not to will, because it is free; but once it wills and while it is willing, it is not able to keep from willing; and it is necessary for it to will, because it is impossible for it both to will and not to will the same thing at the same time.

Now, the will has been given the power to act in such a way that what it wills does occur and what it does not will does not occur. And this act is voluntary or free, because it results from a free will. But this action is also necessary in a double sense: first, because it is compelled to happen by the will; and, second, because what is done cannot at the same time not be done. However, these two kinds of necessity are produced by the freedom of the will, which can prevent them before they come to be. Now, God, who knows all truth and only truth, sees all things just as they are—whether they be free or necessary; and, conversely, as He sees them so they are. It is clear from these considerations that there is no inconsistency in maintaining both that God foreknows all things and that there are many things which, though having before they occur the possibility of never occurring, do actually occur through free will. Yet there is a certain manner in which these things occur by necessity; but this necessity, as I have said, derives from free will.

Chapter IV

There is another way to recognize that not all things which God foreknows, occur by necessity but that some things occur by freedom of will. For this can be seen from the fact that when God wills or causes something, it is undeniable that He knows what He wills or causes and that He foreknows what He shall will or shall cause. This is true whether God's willing and causing are understood in terms of the immutable present of eternity or in terms of the temporal order. (According to the former, nothing is past or future, but everything exists together without any change. In this regard we do not say that God has willed or has caused something or that He shall will or shall cause something; we say only that He does will or does cause something. But when we say that God shall will or shall cause something which we know has not yet been done, we are thinking of God's action in terms of the temporal order.) So, then, if God's knowledge and foreknowledge impose necessity on all the things He knows and foreknows, then He Himself wills and causes nothing freely, but rather wills and causes all things by necessity [since His knowledge, or foreknowledge, imposes necessity upon His own will and also upon created things]. And so whether His willing and causing are understood in terms of the eternal order or in some temporal sense, they would be necessary. But if it is absurd even to suppose that God wills and causes by necessity, then not everything which He knows or foreknows to be or not to be occurs or does not occur by necessity. Therefore, there is nothing which prevents God's knowing or foreknowing something in our volitions and actions as occurring (whether now or in the future) through free choice. Thus, even though it is necessary that what He knows or foreknows should occur, nevertheless many things do occur without necessity and through free will, in the way I explained earlier.

Why should it be thought surprising that in this manner something exists both freely and by necessity, since there are many things which, seen from different points of view, have contrary characteristics? For what could be more opposite than "to come toward" and "to go away from"? Yet we see that when someone goes from one place to another, the same movement is both "coming toward" and "going away from." For in going away from one place he comes toward another. Or, again, if we consider the sun, ever hastening to some part of the heavens in its luminous journey across them, we see that the place from which it withdraws and the place to which it returns are the same. Moreover, we see that all the while the sun is leaving this place it is also approaching it. To those who know the sun's course, it is also clear that with respect to the heavens the sun ever makes its transit from the western sector to the eastern one, whereas with respect to the earth it only moves from east to west. Thus, the sun always moves both counter to the firmament and with the firmament—although more slowly than the firmament—as we notice with regard to all planets.[3] [We see, then, that opposite characteristics may be ascribed to the same thing in different respects.] For this reason there is no inconsistency in maintaining that something is *necessarily* going to happen (simply because it is going to happen) and also that it is not compelled to happen by necessity, except for the necessity which, as I said before, follows free will.

Chapter V

Someone might point to the statement which Job made to God concerning man, "You have established his end, which cannot be escaped" (Job 14:5), and from this try to show, in spite of the fact that people sometimes seem to cause their own deaths by their own free will, that no one can hasten or delay the day of his death. But this would not produce a sound argument against what we have said above. Since God cannot be deceived and since He sees only what is true—whether this results from necessity or from freedom—He is said to have established immutably within Himself something which can be altered with respect to man before it actually comes to pass. Thus, the Apostle Paul says of those who are called to be saints according to God's purpose: "Those whom He foreknew He also predestined to be conformed to the image of His Son, that He might be the firstborn among many brethren. For whom He predestined, them He also called; and whom He called, them He also justified; and whom He justified, them He also glorified" (Rom. 1:7; 8:28, 29). Now, this purpose, according to which these men are called to be saints, is within eternity an immutable purpose, for within eternity there is no past or future but only a present; but in the men themselves this purpose is sometimes mutable because of

3. Anselm is referring to the fact that the sun appears to revolve around the earth from *east to west* (i.e., "with the firmament") once every day. At the same time, the sun actually moves among the stars from *west to east* (i.e., "counter to the firmament"), making one complete circuit of the heavens in a year. Because the sun changes its position in the heavens constantly at a uniform rate, it requires a few more minutes than do the stars to complete its daily apparent revolution about the earth. A similar effect is generally true for the planets as well.

human freedom of choice. For it is not contradictory to say both that within eternity something does occur (never that it has occurred or will occur) and that within time this same event has occurred or will occur. Accordingly, it is not inconsistent to maintain that an event which is unchangeable in eternity may, before it actually occurs in time, be changeable as a result of free will.

Even though nothing exists within eternity except the present, nevertheless this is not a temporal present as we know it but an eternal present in which the whole of time is contained. Just as the temporal present encompasses every place and everything whatsoever that is occurring in these places, so too does the eternal present contain the whole of time and everything which is in time.[4] Thus, when the Apostle declares that God foreknew, predestined, called, justified, and glorified His saints, we must understand that none of these occurs earlier or later than the others for God, but that all of them are together at once within an eternal present. For eternity has its own "simultaneity" and encompasses all the things that occur at the same time and place and that occur at different times and places.

In order to show that he was not using these words in their temporal signification, the same Apostle used verbs in the past tense to refer even to future events. For, temporally speaking, God has not already called, justified, and glorified those who He foreknows are still to be born. From this we can see that for want of a verb that would adequately signify the eternal present, the Apostle used verbs of past tense; for things which are temporally past are altogether immutable, and in this way resemble the eternal present. In this respect the temporal past is more like the eternal present than is the temporal present. For what is temporally past can never be not-past, just as what is eternally present can never be not-present; but all temporally present things which pass away with time do become not-present.

Accordingly, Holy Scripture speaks of everything that occurs through free choice as if it were necessary. In this way it speaks

4. Anselm draws upon Augustine's conception of time—of which *Confessions*, Bk. 11, is a part.

in accordance with the eternal order, where all truth and only truth is present immutably. It does not speak in accordance with the temporal order, wherein our volitions and actions do not exist forever. Indeed, it is not necessary that our volitions and actions exist before such time as they do exist; moreover, it is often not even necessary that they should exist at any time. For example, I am not engaged in writing all the time, nor do I always want to write. Now, when I am not writing or wanting to write, it is not necessary for me to write or to want to write. By the same token there is no necessity that I should ever write or want to write.

A thing's existence in time is so different from its existence in eternity that at a given moment something may not be present in time which is present in eternity, or something may be past in time without being past in eternity, or may be future in time without being future in eternity. When we realize this, we have no basis for denying that something can be mutable in time while being immutable in eternity. Indeed, something's being mutable in time and immutable in eternity is no more contradictory than something's not existing at a certain time but always existing in eternity, or its having been or its going to be in the order of time while being neither past nor future in the order of eternity.

I am not saying that something which always exists in eternity never exists in time, but only that there are moments in time when such a thing does not exist. I would not say, for instance, that my actions of tomorrow never occur at any time; I merely say that they are not occurring today, even though their occurrence is forever present in eternity. Similarly, when we deny of something which was or will be in time that it ever was or will be in eternity, we are not claiming that what was or will be has no existence of any kind in eternity; we are only pointing out that what exists there unceasingly in its own eternal-present mode does not exist there in the past or future mode. There is no contradiction in this. Thus, there is also no contradiction in saying that something is mutable in time, prior to its occurrence, and that it remains immutable in eternity, where nothing exists before or after but everything exists continually. For nothing exists in eternity according to temporal modes. And there exists there even the eternal fact of something's temporal existence and of its being possible not to exist before it actually does come into existence. I think it is sufficiently clear from what I have said that there is no mutual incompatibility whatsoever between the foreknowledge of God and free choice. This is due to the very nature of eternity, which encompasses all time and everything whatsoever that exists at any time.

Chapter VI

Inasmuch as we do not have free choice in all things, we must determine the nature and scope of the freedom of choice which we believe man always has, and we must say something about the nature of choice. For choice and freedom of choice are not the same thing. In many cases we speak of both freedom and choice. We say, for example, that someone is free to speak or to remain silent and that he has the choice of doing whichever he prefers. Freedom and choice are likewise said to be present in many other instances where they are not always present or where they are not necessary to the salvation of our souls. But I am considering only the choice and freedom which are indispensable to man's salvation once he has become able to use them. Now, many people complain bitterly because they think that free choice has nothing to do with their salvation or condemnation, which they regard as solely a matter of necessity following from the foreknowledge of God. Inasmuch as man, after he reaches the age of understanding, cannot be saved without his own justice, we must examine choice and the freedom from which choice is exercised and determine where the seat of justice is. But first we must explain what justice is, and then we can go on to discuss freedom and choice.

Any justice whatever, great or small, is uprightness of will kept for its own sake. And freedom is the ability to keep uprightness of will for its own sake. I think I have already given clear considerations in behalf of these definitions, first in the treatise I published *Concerning Truth* and then again in the treatise *On*

Freedom of Choice. In the latter I showed that this freedom belongs to man naturally and inseparably, even though he does not always use it. I also showed that this freedom is so strong that as long as a man wills to use it nothing can take away the above-mentioned uprightness (that is, the justice) which he possesses. But justice is not a natural possession; in the beginning it was something separable in both the angels in Heaven and man in Paradise. And even now in this life it is separable, not by necessity but by the individual willing of those who possess it. Now, as I said, it is evident that the justice by which a person is just is the uprightness of his will; and this uprightness is in a person only when he wills what God wills him to will. Hence, it is clear that God cannot take a man's uprightness away from him against his will, for God cannot will such a thing.[5] But neither can He will that the man who possesses uprightness should by reason of some necessity desert that uprightness unwillingly. For then He would be willing the man *not* to will that which He wills him *to* will—which is impossible. It follows, therefore, that in this way God wills that the upright will be free to will rightly and to keep its uprightness. And when the will is able actually to do what it wills to do, then it does freely what it does. This, therefore, is another very clear way to see that there are wills which are free in their actions without contradicting the foreknowledge of God—a truth I demonstrated earlier.

Let us now postulate the case of a man in whom there appears (1) an upright, or just, will, (2) freedom of choice, and (3) an actual choice. Let us consider how the upright will might be attacked so as to make it desert uprightness, and how it might keep uprightness by free choice. Let us say that someone wishes in his heart to cling to the truth because he knows that it is right to love truth. He has, then, an upright will, or uprightness of will. We must bear in mind that the will itself is one thing and the uprightness by which it is upright is another. Now, suppose that someone approaches this man and threatens to kill him unless he tells a lie.[6] He now has the choice of either forsaking

5. Cf. DL, 8.
6. Cf. DL, 5.

life in favor of uprightness or deserting uprightness in order to live. This choice, or judgment, is free; for reason, which apprehends uprightness, teaches that uprightness ought always to be cherished for its own sake, and that anything set before the will to entice it to forsake uprightness should be despised. And the function of the will is to choose or not to choose in accordance with what reason apprehends. Indeed, it is mostly to this end that reason and will are given in the highest degree to rational creatures. Wherefore the choice of the will to desert uprightness is not compelled by any necessity, even though the choice is made under pain of death. For even though it is necessary for the person to relinquish either his life or his uprightness, there is no necessity which determines which one he should either keep or forsake. Indeed, in such a case the will alone determines which one he keeps; and when a man acts solely through the choice of his will, nothing is done by force of necessity. But it is obvious that a person who is under no necessity of forsaking uprightness of will does not lack the ability to keep uprightness, that is, does not lack freedom. For this ability is always free. And freedom, as I have said, is the ability to keep uprightness of will for its own sake. Because rational nature possesses this freedom, it is said to have both free choice and free will.

Chapter VII

We have still another question to consider. Since God is believed to know or foreknow all things, does His knowledge derive from the things He knows or do the things derive their existence from His knowledge? If God derives His knowledge from things, it follows that they are prior to His knowledge and thus are not from Him, for they cannot come from God except through His knowledge. But if, on the other hand, everything that exists receives its being from the knowledge of God, then God is the Author and Creator of evil and is unjust in punishing evil creatures. This belief, however, we do not accept.

The issue can easily be resolved if we first recognize that the good which is justice is really something—whereas the evil which

is injustice altogether lacks existence. I have shown this most
clearly in the treatise on *The Fall of Satan* and in the treatise
entitled *On the Virgin Conception and Original Sin*. Injustice is
neither a quality nor an action nor a being, but merely the absence
of due justice; and injustice is located only in the will, where
justice ought to be. Now, each rational nature and every action
of that nature is called just or unjust according to whether the
will is just or unjust. Certainly, every quality, every action, and
anything whatsoever that has being comes from God, who is the
source of all justice and from whom comes no injustice. God,
then, is the Author of all things that proceed from a just or
unjust will—viz., good and evil deeds. But, whereas God causes
the existence and the goodness of good things, He causes only the
existence, and not the evil, of evil things. For a thing to be just,
or good, is for it to be something; but for something to be unjust,
or evil, is not for it to be anything. If being good, or just, is having justice, which is something, then being evil, or unjust, is not
having the justice one ought to have. And this not-having is
not something; for, although justice is something, injustice, as I
have said, is nothing.

Now, there is another kind of good, which we call *benefit*
(*commodum*); and we call the corresponding evil *disadvantage*
(*incommodum*). This evil is in some cases nothing, as with
blindness; but sometimes it is something, as in the case of pain.
When this evil is something, we do not deny that God causes it,
because He is "the One who makes peace and creates evil" (Is.
45:7). For He creates hardships and uses them to try and to
purify the just, and to punish the unjust. We may be sure,
however, that the evil according to which a man is called unjust,
namely, injustice, is never something. Nor is it anything for a
thing to be unjust. Now, even as God does not cause injustice,
neither does He cause anything to be unjust. But He does cause
all actions and all movements, in that He causes the things from
which, out of which, by which, and in which they come to be.
Every creature possesses only such power to will or to do anything as God has given. And the willing itself—which is sometimes just, sometimes unjust—is nothing other than using the

will and the ability to will which God gives. Thus, willing, in so far as it is, is something good and is from God. Now, when the ability to will is used rightly, it is something good and just; but when it is not used rightly, then in this respect (and only in this respect) is it something evil and unjust. Existing rightly is something and is from God. When a person uses a sword, for instance, or uses language, or the power of speaking, it is the same sword or language or power whether he uses it correctly or incorrectly. The same is true of the will. As with reason, which we use for reasoning, so the will is not one thing when we use it correctly and something different when we use it incorrectly. A substance or an action is said to be just or unjust according to the will. But what the will essentially is, is neither more nor less when it is just than when it is unjust. Thus, God causes both the essential being and the goodness of all good wills and good works. And He causes the essential being of all evil wills and evil works, but He does not cause their being evil. For even as a thing's being is from God alone, so its rightness is from Him alone.

Injustice, which is the absence of the uprightness we are discussing, is located only in the will of rational creatures, who ought always to have justice. But why does a rational creature not have that justice which he ought always to have, and how does God cause good things solely by His goodness and evil things solely through the fault of man or Satan? And how does man do good through free choice, under the guidance of grace, and yet do evil by the working of his own will alone? What part can God play in evil works without being culpable, and how are we to understand man's praiseworthiness in performing good works, when we clearly see that his good works must be attributed to God and his evil works to himself? I think that with the help of God these issues will become much clearer when we come to deal with the question of grace and free choice. For the moment, I shall simply say that the evil angel does not possess justice, because he abandoned it and has not since regained it. But man is without justice because in his first parents he rejected it; and in the time since then he either has not recovered it or, having once recovered it, he has once again rejected it.

I think that with the help of God's grace we have now shown that both the foreknowledge of God and free choice exist at the same time. If what we have said is carefully considered, it will be clear that this compatibility is not impossible. And against this truth there is no objection which cannot be satisfactorily answered.

Question Two:
On Predestination and Free Choice

Chapter I

Trusting in God, who has led us every step thus far, let us now attempt to resolve the conflict which seems to exist between predestination and free choice. Through the things which we have expounded above we have already made considerable progress with this problem. This fact will become quite evident in the ensuing chapters.

It seems that predestination is the same thing as foreordination or predetermination; and so God is understood to foreordain anything that He predestines—or, in other words, to determine that it shall occur. But it seems that what God determines to be going to exist, necessarily must be going to exist. Whatever God predestines, then, necessarily will be. So, if God predestines both the good and the evil actions which occur, then every action occurs by necessity and nothing occurs through free choice. If, on the other hand, God predestines only good actions, then only good actions occur by necessity and there is free choice only in regard to evil things—a view which is completely absurd. Consequently, God does not predestine only good deeds. Now, if the good works that make men just occur through free choice without being predestined, then God does not predestine all the good works which make men just. In this case He would not predestine men who are just through their works of free choice. So, then, God did not foreknow them either, because "whom He foreknew, them He also predestined" (Rom. 8:29). But it is false to say that there are good works or just men that God does not foreknow. Therefore, it is not the case that certain good works done by free choice alone, justify men; rather, only those good works which God predestines justify men. Thus, if God predestines everything and if everything that is predestined occurs by necessity, then since nothing which occurs through free choice occurs by necessity, it seems to follow that as long as predestination remains in effect there is no free choice. Or else it seems to follow that if we can establish some area of free choice, then in that area predestination is inoperative.

Chapter II

Before I answer this question, it is especially important to notice that predestination does not apply only to good actions. It can also be said to apply to evil actions—just as God can be said to do the evil deeds which He does not Himself do but which He permits to occur. For example, God is said to harden a man's heart when He does not soften it, and He is said to lead a man into temptation when He does not deliver him from it. So, then, it is the same sort of thing to say that God predestines evil men and their evil works when He does not correct these men and their evil works. But in a more special way God is said to foreknow and predestine good things, because, as I said above, He causes both their being and their being good—whereas in evil things He causes only their essential being, not their being evil. We should also understand that like *fore*knowledge, *pre*destination is not properly attributed to God. For there is no before or after in God, but all things are present to Him at once.

Chapter III

Let us now consider whether some things can be predestined to occur through free choice. We must never suppose that there is a conflict between God's foreknowledge and predestination, for

God predestines a thing exactly as He foreknows it. When dealing with the question of foreknowledge, we saw clearly that there is no contradiction in saying that some things are foreknown to occur through free choice. From this, both reason and plain truth teach us likewise that there is no contradiction in saying that some things are predestined to occur through free choice. For God neither foreknows nor predestines anyone to be just by necessity. Anyone who does not keep justice by his free will does not really have justice. Therefore, although it is necessary that what is foreknown and what is predestined should occur, nevertheless some of the things foreknown and predestined do not occur by the necessity which precedes a thing and causes it, but only by the necessity which (as I said above) follows the thing's occurrence. For, although God predestines these things, He does not cause them by compelling the will or by restraining it, but by leaving it to its own power. But although man's will uses its own power, it does nothing which God by His grace does not do in good actions, and which in evil actions He does, not by His grace but by the fault of the human will. As I promised, these things will become clearer when we speak of grace. Now, just as foreknowledge cannot be mistaken and foreknows only the truth in the way in which it will occur—whether freely or by necessity— so also predestination cannot be altered and predestines a thing in the way in which it is foreknown. And just as what is foreknown is immutable in eternity but can nevertheless be changed in time at any moment before it comes to be, the same is true of all things which are predestined.

It should be clear now to anyone who carefully considers what I have said that predestination does not exclude free choice and that free choice is not opposed to predestination. Indeed, all the foregoing arguments that were used to show that free choice is not inconsistent with foreknowledge show equally clearly that free choice is compatible with predestination. Thus, when something happens through the free operation of the will, as when a man inflicts an injury upon another and is killed by him in return, we see how unreasonable it is for people to say, as they do so often and with such clamor, "God foreknew and predestined that this act should occur in the way it did; so it was committed by necessity and couldn't have been otherwise." After all, neither the man who inflicts the injury nor the one who avenges himself acts from necessity. Both act solely through the will; for had they not willed freely what they did, neither would have done what he did.

Question Three: Concerning Grace and Free Choice

Chapter I

We must now consider the question of grace and free choice, and we must do so with the help of this very grace. The question arises from the fact that Holy Scripture speaks in places as if free choice could contribute nothing to salvation, intimating that salvation comes through grace alone—while in other passages it speaks as if our salvation depended entirely upon our free will. For example, the Lord says concerning grace, "Without me you can do nothing" (John 15:5), and "No one comes to me unless my Father draws him" (John 6:44). And the Apostle Paul says, "What do you have that you have not received?" (I Cor. 4:7). He also says, speaking of God, "He has mercy on whom He will have mercy and whom He will He hardens" (Rom. 9:18). Also, "It is not of him who wills nor of him who runs, but of God, who shows mercy" (Rom. 9:16). Besides these there are many other passages which seem to attribute our good works and our salvation to grace alone apart from free choice. Moreover, many people even claim that they can show by experience that man is not at all aided by free choice. They see a great many individuals who make an immense effort of body and mind but are hindered by some difficulty, or even impossibility, so that they either make no progress or, having made great progress, suddenly and irretrievably fall back.

Scripture, however, teaches that we do have free choice. For God says through Isaiah, "If you are willing and will hearken unto me, you shall eat the good things of the land" (Is. 1:19).

And David says, ''Who is the man who wishes life, who loves many days so that he may see good things? Keep your tongue from evil and your lips from speaking guile; turn away from evil and do good'' (Ps. 34:12–14). And the Lord says in the Gospel, ''Come unto me, all of you who are laboring and are heavily laden, and I will give you rest. Take my yoke upon you, and learn from me, for I am meek and lowly in heart, and you shall find rest for your souls'' (Matt. 11:28, 29). There are countless other passages which seem to urge free choice to good works and to reproach it for spurning their admonitions. Now, divine authority would never do this if it knew that there were no freedom of will in man. Nor would it be possible for God justly to reward good and evil men according to their merits if they had done nothing good or evil through free choice.

Since we find in Holy Scripture certain passages which seem to favor the doctrine of grace alone, and other passages which seem to hold that free choice can stand alone without grace, there have been certain arrogant men who have thought that the whole efficacy of moral virtue derives entirely from freedom of choice— while in our day there are many who have completely given up on the idea that there is such a thing as free choice. In this question, therefore, it will be our purpose to show that free choice exists together with grace and actually cooperates with it in many things—just as we discovered earlier that free choice is compatible with foreknowledge and predestination.

Chapter II

We should bear in mind that just as in our discussion of this question up to this point we have not been concerned with free choice in general but only with that free choice which is indispensable to meriting salvation after one has reached the age of understanding, so now we are concerned only with that grace which is indispensable for man's salvation. Every creature exists by grace, because he has been created by grace. Besides this, there are many good things in this life which man does not need for salvation, but which God gives him by grace. Now, the harmony that we are seeking does not appear in infants who die after they have been baptized but before they have been able to use their free choice, because in them grace alone effects salvation without any exercise of free choice on their part. For it is also by grace that others are given the will to let their faith assist these infants. Therefore, we must direct our inquiry toward those who have reached the age of understanding, because the issue deals only with them.

There is no doubt that all those in this number who are saved are saved through justice, because eternal life is promised to the just. For "The just will live forever and their reward is with the Lord" (Wisd. of Sol. 5:15). Sacred authority often points out that justice is uprightness of will. It suffices to cite only one example of this. David says, "The Lord will not cast off His people nor forsake His inheritance until judgment shall return to justice" (Ps. 94:14, 15). But after he had said this he asked the following question in order to teach us what justice is: "And who is conformed to justice?" To this he replies, "Everyone who is upright in heart," which means everyone who is upright in will. For, though we *believe* and *understand* by the heart—even as we *will* by the heart—the Holy Spirit does not judge a man to have an upright heart when he believes or understands rightly but does not will rightly. This is because such a man does not use the uprightness of faith and of understanding for that end for which they have been given to rational creatures, namely, for upright willing. No one should be said to have right understanding when he does not use this understanding to will rightly. Nor should anyone be said to have faith, except a dead faith, when he does not use this faith for the purpose for which it is given, namely, to will upright deeds. For this reason we are right to understand David as identifying the upright in heart with the upright in will. But, lest someone suppose divine authority to teach that a man is just, or upright, when he keeps uprightness of will as a means to something else, we insist that justice is uprightness of will kept for its own sake. For a man who keeps uprightness only for the sake of something else really loves not uprightness but that object for the sake of which he is keeping uprightness. Accordingly, we should never call this man just, and we should never say that such uprightness is justice.

When we were dealing with the relationship of foreknowledge to free choice we showed by a particular example that it is possible for this uprightness, which I call justice, to coexist with free choice. Through this example one can plainly see that the same thing can be true of many other cases. Thus, if we can show that no creature can obtain uprightness without grace, the harmony we are seeking between grace and free choice in the work of saving man will be manifest.

Chapter III

There is certainly no doubt that the will wills rightly only because it itself is upright. No man's sight is acute because he sees clearly; rather, a man sees clearly because his sight is acute. So, too, the will is not upright because it wills rightly, but rather it wills rightly because it is itself upright. There is no doubt that when a man wills this uprightness he wills rightly. Therefore, he wills uprightness only because his will is upright. But it is the same for the will to be upright and for it to have uprightness. Thus, it is clear that a man wills uprightness only because he has uprightness. I do not deny that an upright will wills an uprightness which it does not yet have when it wills more uprightness than it already has. But I maintain that the will can will no uprightness if it has no uprightness at all by which to will it.

Let us now consider whether someone who does not have this uprightness can obtain it in some way from himself. If he has it from himself, he must have it either by willing it or without willing it. Now, no one is able by willing uprightness to obtain it through his own efforts, since he cannot will it unless he already has it. And no sound mind can believe that someone who does not have uprightness of will should be able without willing it to obtain it by himself. Therefore, there is no way for a creature to have uprightness from himself. But neither can a creature have it from another creature. For it is just as impossible for one creature to give to another the necessary means of salvation as it

is for one creature to save another. It follows, therefore, that
only by the grace of God can a creature have the uprightness of
will that I have been discussing. We have demonstrated, however, that this uprightness can be kept through free choice. So
with the bountiful help of God we have found that His grace
works harmoniously with free choice for the salvation of man.
Thus, grace alone can save man when there is no free choice
exercised, as in the case of infants. But in those who have
reached the age of understanding, grace always helps the natural
free choice by giving to the will the uprightness which it can
keep through free choice—for without grace free choice can do
nothing effective for salvation.

And, although God does not give His grace to everyone, since
"He has mercy on whom He will have mercy, and whom He will
He hardens" (Rom. 9:18), nevertheless He does not give grace
to anyone as a reward for some antecedent merit, for "Who has
first given to God and shall be recompensed by Him?" (Rom.
11:35). If, however, the will through free choice keeps what it has
received and in this way merits either an increment of received
justice, or even power for a good will, or some reward, then all
these are the fruit of the first grace. The bestowing of these
rewards, then, really amounts to the giving of "grace for grace"
(John 1:16). Consequently, everything must be attributed to
grace, for willing and running are "not of him who wills nor of
him who runs, but of God, who shows mercy" (Rom. 9:16). For
the following statement from Scripture is addressed to everyone
except God alone: "What do you have that you have not received? And if you have received it, why do you glory as if you
had not received it?" (I Cor. 4:7).

Chapter IV

I believe that in the treatise *On Freedom of Choice* I explained
how a free will which has received the gift of uprightness is not
compelled by any necessity to forsake uprightness, but how it
yields willingly and not without consent when it is assailed by
difficulties. Now, because grace helps the will in such a multitude

of ways, I shall not be able to enumerate all of them. But it will be worthwhile for me to say something about the ways in which the received grace helps free choice to keep uprightness after the will has received it.

It is obvious that no one can keep this received uprightness without willing to do so. But a person cannot will uprightness unless he possesses it. And the only way he can possess it is by grace. Now, just as no one receives uprightness unless grace precedes it and enables him, so no one keeps uprightness unless the same grace follows it and helps him. Even though the keeping of uprightness, when it is kept, is done through free choice, this keeping must not be attributed to free choice so much as to grace; for free choice possesses uprightness only through prevenient grace and keeps it only through subsequent grace.

Grace so follows its own gift that it fails to bestow this gift of uprightness, whether it be great or small, only when free choice by willing something else deserts the uprightness it has received. For this uprightness is never separated from the will except when the will chooses something else that is incompatible with uprightness—as happens, for instance, when someone who receives the uprightness of willing sobriety throws it away by immoderately willing the pleasure of drinking. When a man does this, he does it of his own will; so through his own fault he loses the grace which he has received. When free choice is assailed by a temptation to forsake the uprightness it has received, grace still helps the will by reducing or completely nullifying the power of the temptation besetting it or by increasing the will's affection for uprightness. Furthermore, since all things are subject to the governance of God, then everything that happens to man which helps free choice to receive or to keep the uprightness we are talking about ought to be imputed to grace.

I have said that all justice is uprightness of will kept for its own sake. It follows from this that everyone who has this uprightness has justice; and since everyone who has justice is just, everyone who has uprightness is just. Nevertheless, I do not believe that eternal life has been promised to all who are just but only to those who are just without being at all unjust. For it is the latter who are properly and absolutely said to be just and upright in heart. There are some people who are just in one respect and unjust in another, such as the man who is both chaste and envious. The happiness of the just is not given to people like this. For, as true happiness exists without any deficiency, so it is given only to the person who is just without being unjust in any way. The happiness promised to just men will be like that enjoyed by the angels of God. Thus, since there is no injustice in the good angels, no one who has any injustice will be admitted to their company. It is not the purpose of our present discourse to show how a man can become free of injustice; but we know that by the grace of God and through holy endeavors this is possible for the Christian.

Chapter V

Anyone who carefully considers what has been said will recognize clearly that when Holy Scripture says something in favor of grace, it is not flatly denying the role of free choice. And when Scripture says something in favor of free choice, it does not exclude grace—as if grace alone or free choice alone were sufficient for man's salvation, as those who pose this question think. The divine words should be understood to mean that neither grace alone nor free choice alone can accomplish man's salvation (with the exception of what I said about the salvation of infants).

For when the Lord says "Without me you can do nothing" (John 15:5), He certainly is not saying "Your free choice is of no avail to you" but only "It is of no avail without my grace." When we read, "It is not of him who wills nor of him who runs, but of God, who shows mercy" (Rom. 9:16), Scripture is not denying that free choice does something useful in a man who wills or runs; it is rather signifying that the willing and the running are not to be attributed to free choice but to grace. For "It is not of him who wills nor of him who runs" should be understood as referring to the act of willing and the act of running. The same sort of thing happens when someone gives a garment to a naked man to whom he owes nothing, but who is unable to obtain any clothing by himself. Even though the naked man has the power to use or not to use the garment he receives, nevertheless if he actually puts it on, then the fact that he is clothed should not be imputed to him but to the man who gave it to him.[7] Wherefore, we can say, "The fact that he is clothed is not of him who is clothed, but of him who shows mercy, that is, of him who gives the garment." This could be said much more emphatically of the one who gave the garment if he had also given the ability to keep and to use it. This is the case with God. When He gives man the uprightness we have so often mentioned, He also gives him the ability to keep and to use it; for before He gave man uprightness He gave him free choice for the purpose of keeping and using uprightness. Now, if, since no one owed the naked man anything, everyone had refused to give him any clothing, or if he himself had thrown the garment away after receiving it, then his nakedness could be imputed only to himself. Thus, when God gives the ability to will or to run to someone conceived and born in sin, to whom He owes nothing but punishment, this ability "is not of him who wills nor of him who runs, but of God, who shows mercy." As for the one who does not accept that grace or, having once accepted it, spurns it: it is his own fault, not God's, that he continues in his hardness and his iniquity.

The same interpretation—namely, that free choice is not excluded—must be given to other passages in which Scripture speaks in favor of grace. Similarly, when the divine words speak in such a way that they seem to attribute man's salvation solely to free choice, no one should understand this to mean that grace is excluded from this work. Even though offspring are naturally begotten only by a father and through a mother, still no account of procreation excludes either father or mother from the generation of children. Similarly, grace and free choice are not incompatible but work together for the justification and salvation of man.

7. Cf. DCD, 1.

Chapter VI

Now, when Scripture appears to exhort free choice in various matters to will and to work uprightly, one wonders why it summons men to right willing and why it condemns those who do not obey, since no one can have or receive uprightness unless God gives him grace. We should note that whereas the earth produces innumerable herbs and trees which have no nutritive value for man (while some may even kill him), and whereas these grow without having to be cared for by men, the earth brings forth the vegetation we need most for bodily nourishment only when someone plants seeds and labors strenuously over them. In the same way, without effort or needing to be taught, human hearts freely germinate, as it were, thoughts and inclinations which are entirely useless—perhaps even harmful—for salvation. But, unless a unique seed is planted within and unless that seed is laboriously cultivated, human hearts never conceive or generate the thoughts and inclinations which we cannot do without if we are to make any progress toward the salvation of our souls. For this reason the Apostle calls those men on whom such care is lavished "God's husbandry" (I Cor. 3:9). The seed of this husbandry is the word of God—or, better, not the word itself but the meaning which the word carries. For the sound of the word apart from its meaning accomplishes nothing in a man's heart. Moreover, the seed of upright willing comprises not just the meaning of the word of God but also every sense and understanding of uprightness that the human mind can apprehend by hearing, reading, reasoning, or in any way whatsoever.

No one can will what he does not first conceive in his heart. Now, to will to believe what should be believed is to will uprightly. But no one can will this if he does not know what should be believed. For when the Apostle proclaimed, "Whosoever shall call upon the name of the Lord shall be saved," he added, "How shall they call on Him in whom they have not believed? And how shall they believe in Him of whom they have not heard? And how shall they hear without a preacher? And how shall they preach except they be sent?'' (Rom. 10:13–15). And a little later he says, "Therefore faith comes by hearing and hearing by the word of Christ.'' We should understand the statement "faith comes by hearing'' to mean that faith comes from what the mind apprehends or conceives through hearing, not in the sense that the mind's conception alone produces faith in man, but in the sense that there can be no faith without some conception. Faith comes into being when, by grace, uprightness of willing is added to the conception, because then a man believes what he hears. "And hearing comes by the word of Christ,'' that is, by the word of those who preach Christ. Now, there are no preachers unless they are sent. But the fact that they are sent is due to grace. Therefore, preaching is grace, since what derives from grace is also a grace; and hearing is a grace, and the understanding which comes from hearing is a grace, and uprightness of willing is a grace. But sending, preaching, hearing, and understanding come to naught unless the will wills what the mind understands. But the will cannot do this unless it has received uprightness. For one wills uprightly when he wills what he ought to will. Thus, what the mind apprehends or conceives through hearing the word, is the seed planted in the mind by preaching; and uprightness is the growth which God gives. For without God there would be no growth, for "neither he who plants nor he who waters is anything, but only God, who gives the growth'' (I Cor. 3:7).

Just as in the beginning God miraculously—without using seeds or the help of a cultivator—made wheat and other things to grow from the earth for the nourishment of men, so also miraculously—without the use of human teaching—He made the Gospels and the hearts of the apostles and prophets rich in the seeds which give salvation. From these seeds we receive whatever seeds of salvation we sow in God's husbandry for the nourishment of our souls—just as we now possess only from among the first seeds of the earth those seeds which we cultivate for the nourishment of our bodies. Nothing that we preach is effective for spiritual salvation except what Holy Scripture, made fruitful by the miracle of the Holy Spirit, has brought forth and contains.

For, if at times we cannot clearly show that a view we affirm by reason is also in Scripture, or if we cannot prove it from what Scripture says, then in one way we can still learn through Scripture whether such a view should be accepted or rejected. For Scripture opposes no truth and favors no falsity. So, if a view is adopted on the basis of a clear reason and if this view is not contradicted in any part of Scripture, then it may be said to be supported by the authority of Scripture, for Scripture does not contradict what is said by reason. But, even though our reason may seem unassailable to us, we should not believe that it is supported by any truth if Scripture is obviously opposed to our understanding. Thus, when Holy Scripture either affirms clearly or does not at all deny what reason teaches, it contains the authority for all the truth which reason apprehends.

Let us now consider some examples which show how the word is the seed. When people hear it said, "If you are willing and will hearken unto me" (Is. 1:19), they understand and believe that what is meant is willing and hearing, or obeying. For a person who hears but does not obey cannot really be said to hear. One cannot obey, however, unless he wills. Now, to will to obey is to will uprightly. But no one is able to will uprightly unless he has uprightness of will; and a person has such uprightness only by grace. Moreover, uprightness in willing something is given only to the person who understands both what it is to will and what he ought to will. We see, therefore, that the word, "If you are willing and will hearken unto me," is in no way a seed that bears fruit by itself without uprightness being added to it; and uprightness is given only by means of such seeds.

Similarly, when God says "Be converted to me" (Is. 45:22), these words are a seed which bears no fruit as long as God does not turn the will of man toward willing conversion. A man thinks of conversion when he hears the command "Be converted"; and without the seed of this word no one can will to be converted. The command, "Be converted," is addressed even to those who are already converted, with the idea either that they become converted even more or that they preserve what they have already become. Those who say "Convert us, O Lord" (Ps.

85 :4) are already in some sense converted; for anyone who wills to be converted already has an upright will. On the basis of the conversion they have already received, they are praying that their conversion may grow—in the same way that those who were already believers once asked, "Increase our faith" (Luke 17 :5). It is as if both the former and the latter were praying "Increase in us what you have given; perfect what you have begun." What I have shown to be true in these instances also applies in similar cases.

So, then, just as the earth does not without seeds naturally bring forth those things which are most necessary to the health of our bodies, neither does the soil of the human heart bring forth the fruit of faith or of justice without the appropriate seeds. Furthermore, even though God does not give growth to all the seeds that are planted, nevertheless, farmers continue to plant seeds in the hope of reaping some small harvest. Similarly, God instructs His workers most urgently to plant the seed of His word in hope, even though God does not cause every seed of faith and justice to germinate. We have now shown, I think, why it is not superfluous to invite men to faith in Christ and to the things which faith demands, even though not everyone accepts the invitation.

Chapter VII

I have said that it is even possible to ask why those who do not accept the Word of God should be blamed, since they are unable to accept it unless grace directs their wills. For the Lord says, speaking about the Holy Spirit, "He will accuse the world of sin because they do not believe in me" (John 16 :8, 9). Although it may be difficult to reply to this question, I ought not to keep to myself what insight God grants me. We should note that the inability which results from a fault does not, so long as the fault remains, excuse the man who has the inability. Even in infants, therefore, God demands that human nature have the justice which it received in its first parents and which was accompanied by the ability of every future generation to keep justice. So the inability to have justice does not excuse human nature, for human nature fell into this inability through a fault. The inability of human nature to have justice consists in its not having what it cannot regain by itself [viz., justice]. Human nature fell into this inability because it freely deserted what it was able to keep. Therefore, since it deserted justice by sinning, the inability which it brought upon itself by sinning is counted as sin. In those who are not baptized, not only the inability to have justice but even the inability to understand it is counted as sin, for this inability has also resulted from sin.

We can also reasonably assert that the diminishment and corruption of the dignity, strength, and beauty of human nature's original condition is imputed to it as a fault. In so far as it was able, human nature diminished the honor and glory of God by sinning. Indeed, the wisdom of an artist is proclaimed and praised according to the dignity of his work. Now, human nature is the precious work of God, and He should have been glorified for it. Therefore, to the extent that human nature itself diminished and degraded that work in its own being, to this degree it dishonored God by its own fault. And this fault is imputed to it as such a grave sin that only the death of God is able to blot it out.

On account of the sin of Adam we are subject, like the brute animals, to those passions or appetites which the Apostle calls "the flesh" and "concupiscence" (Rom. 7:7, 8). He reveals that he himself experienced these desires against his will; for he says "What I hate, that I do" (Rom. 7:15)—by which he means "I unwillingly have covetous desires." Sacred authority shows us quite clearly that these passions and appetites are to be counted as sin. Certainly when the Lord says of the passion of anger, even when it occurs without words or actions, "Whoever is angry with his brother will be answerable for it at the judgment" (Matt. 5:22), He shows clearly that the blame for such anger is no trifling matter but is of such gravity that it is followed by the condemnation of death. It is as if He had said, "Whoever does what man ought not to do and what man would not do had he not sinned, ought to be removed from the midst of men.'' Furthermore, Paul declares of those who unwillingly experience the desires of the flesh (that is, experience concupiscent desires), ''There is no condemnation to those who are in Christ Jesus, who walk not according to the flesh'' (that is, to those who do not consent to the flesh willingly) (Rom. 8:1). Now, there is no doubt that he is signifying that condemnation will follow for those who are not in Christ, as often as they feel the desires of the flesh, even if they do not walk according to the flesh. For man was so made that he ought not to feel these desires—just as he ought never (as I said) to feel anger. Therefore, anyone who diligently considers what I have said will have no doubt that the men who, because of their own fault, cannot receive the Word of God will be rightly blamed for it.

Chapter VIII

As regards those to whom the grace of Christian faith is given: just as in baptism the original injustice with which they are born is removed, so also in baptism there is forgiven all guilt of inability and of all the corruption which was incurred as a result of the sin of the first parent and through which God is dishonored. For even though the corruption and the appetites which are the penalty of sin are not immediately erased by baptism, no guilt which was in them before baptism is charged to them after baptism; nor is any transgression imputed to them after baptism except that which they commit by their own will. It appears from this that the corruption and evil which were the penalty of sin and which still remain after baptism are not in themselves sins. For injustice alone is a sin in itself. Until injustice has been remitted, the things which follow from injustice are considered sins by reason of their cause. For if they were [properly] sins they would be blotted out in baptism, where all sins are washed away by the blood of Christ.[8] Moreover, were they properly called sins they would be sins even in the brute animals. For on account of sin human nature endures these penalties which make it resemble the nature of the brute animals.

8. Cf. DCV, 4.

There is something else which can be recognized in the first sin of human nature and which we ought greatly to fear. Man is a "wind that goes out but does not return" (Ps. 78 :39). For this reason, after he freely falls (we are speaking for the moment only of voluntary sins), there is no way that he can rise up again unless grace uplifts him. Unless he is sustained by God's mercy, he is plunged down through his own doing into the bottomless abyss (or measureless depth) of sin, from one sin to another, in such a way that even the good becomes something hateful to him and something that will mean death for him. Thus it is that the Lord says to the apostles, "If the world hate you, know that it hated me before it hated you" (John 15 :18). And the Apostle says, "We are a sweet savor to God," "among some the savor of death unto death, but among others the savor of life unto life" (II Cor. 2 :15, 16). It is because of this that Scripture says of God, "To whom He will He shows mercy, and whom He will He hardens" (Rom. 9 :18). But God does not have mercy equally on all those to whom He shows mercy; nor does He harden equally all the men He hardens.

Chapter IX

Another question has to do with why the penalty of sin remains with us in this life after the sin itself has been blotted out. Although I do not propose to deal with this question now, I will say briefly that if the faithful were immediately transformed by baptism or martyrdom into the state of incorruption, merits would vanish and men would be saved without any merit (except for the first Christians, who would have believed before having witnessed an example of this transformation). This would mean that faith and hope would vanish. But without faith and hope no one of the age of understanding can merit the Kingdom of God. Now, faith and hope relate to things which are not seen. If men were to see people who had been converted to Christ pass over immediately into the state of incorruptibility, there would be no one who could even will to reject such a visible happiness. Therefore, so that we might obtain the happiness which we desire in a more glorious way—namely, through the merit of faith and of hope—we continue in our present state as long as we remain in this life. Though our present state came about as a result of sin, it is no longer counted as sin.

Lastly, the happiness which Adam had in Paradise before he sinned has not been promised to us through baptism and the Christian faith. What has been promised is the happiness which he was to have had after the Celestial City, which is to be filled with men and angels, had become filled with the number of men who were to be taken up to make its number perfect.[9] In the Celestial City there will be no human procreation as there would have been in Paradise. So, if converts to Christ immediately passed over into that state of incorruptibility, there would be no men left from among whom the perfect number could be gathered; for no one would be able to resist rushing for the happiness he would then see. In my opinion this is what the Apostle means when, speaking of those "who have worked justice" "through faith," he says: "And all these, approved by the witness of their faith, have not received the promise, since God is providing something better for us, so that they should not be made perfect without us" (Heb.11:33, 39–40). If someone were to ask what is the better thing that God has provided for us out of their not having received the promise, I see no answer more fitting than what I have said above, namely: if the happiness promised to the just is not delayed for those who have already been approved, then merit would vanish in the lives of those who would learn of this fact through experience rather than through faith. Also, the process of human propagation by which we have been born would come to a halt, since all men would run off after that incorruptibility which they would then be able to see. Therefore, God provided a great good for us when He delayed reception of the promise for the saints, who are already approved by the witness of their faith. He did this both that we might be propagated and that faith might remain, so that through faith

9. Cf. Anselm's discussion in DCD, 5, 23; CDH, I, 16–18. Note also D. P. Henry's "Numerically Definite Reasoning in the *Cur Deus Homo*," *Dominican Studies,* 6(1953), 48–55.

we might merit the promise together with them and might be made perfect together with them.

There is another reason why the baptized and the martyrs do not immediately become incorruptible. Suppose there were a master who had proposed to endow one of his servants with great honors at some future date. But then the master severely chastises his servant for some fault for which the servant is completely unable to render satisfaction by his own efforts. After this chastisement the master at a designated time is going to cast him into a dreadful prison where he will be afflicted with grievous punishments. Suppose further that there is someone else who is influential with the master and who reconciles the servant by making satisfaction for him. Now, the stripes, which the guilty servant deservedly received before satisfaction was rendered and while he was still at fault, are not wiped out; but the larger torments, which he has not yet been made to suffer, are averted by the reconciliation which occurs beforehand. And the honors which he was going to receive in due time had he not sinned and which he was going to be deprived of after sinning, had he not been reconciled—these honors are given to him without alteration, as originally planned, because of the complete satisfaction. If he had been disinherited of these honors before reconciliation (as he was to be irreparably disinherited after he was at fault had he not been reconciled), then reconciliation would have been of no assistance. But since he could not be deprived of an honor which he did not yet have and to which he had no right, reconciliation can occur before this disinheritance and prevent it, provided the servant while lying in the agony of his stripes and awaiting healing does two things: vow in word and in heart that he will improve and be faithful to his master, and, second, fulfill his vow.

This is analogous to the relationship between God and man. When human nature first sinned, it was lashed with a twofold penalty. First, it would naturally produce as descendants only children of such character as we see being born; second, it would after this life be barred from the Kingdom of God, for which it had been created, and would be banished forever to Hell. This was to happen unless someone reconciled human nature, for human nature does not have the ability to reconcile itself. But the only one who can reconcile human nature is Christ. Human nature is born with sin and its penalty in all infants who are naturally begotten. When human nature enters the state of reconciliation the penalty which it received before reconciliation deservedly remains. But the torments which it was going to suffer in Hell are remitted for those whom Christ has redeemed. And the Kingdom of God into which men were to have been received in due time, after their sojourn in the earthly Paradise, will be given to them provided they persevere to the end in the faith which they promise in baptism.

Chapter X

Some men think that they can prove from experience that free choice can do nothing, for they see many people making an enormous effort to live a good life, but who by reason of some alleged impossibility obstructing them either have no success or, after having some success, irretrievably fall back. However, the fact that some men think this way does not destroy what we have rationally demonstrated, namely, that free choice is capable of accomplishing something with the aid of grace. I think the fact that those who make this great effort either do not make any progress or, having made some progress, fall back is due not to an impossibility but to an obstacle—which is sometimes grave and other times easily overcome. It is very often our habit to say about what we can perform only with difficulty that it is impossible for us. But whoever attentively considers any movement of his own will, shall see from his own situation that he can never desert uprightness of will, which he has received by grace, unless he wills something else which he cannot will at the same time he is willing uprightness.[10] He certainly does not do this through a lack of ability to keep uprightness—the very ability which constitutes freedom of choice. Rather, he wills this other thing

10. Anselm argues this point more fully in DCD, 3.

because he lacks the will to keep uprightness. He does not essentially lack the will for uprightness, but he lacks it because willing something other than uprightness drives out the will for uprightness.

Chapter XI

Since the foregoing consideration refers above all to the will, I think it will be worthwhile to say something further about the will. In our bodies we have five separate senses and also various members, each of which we use like instruments. Our members and our senses are all adapted to their own particular use. For example, our hands are suited for grasping, our feet for walking, our tongues for speaking, and our sight for seeing. In the same manner there are certain powers within the soul, which the soul uses as instruments for appropriate functions. There is, for instance, reason in the soul, which the soul uses as an instrument for reasoning; there is also will, which it uses for willing. Now, reason and will do not comprise the whole soul, but each is something in the soul. Inasmuch as every instrument has its nature, its aptitudes (*aptitudines*),[11] and its uses, let us distinguish within the will (according to the categories we have just drawn) the instrument, its aptitudes, and its uses. The aptitudes of the will we can call affections (*affectiones*). For the instrument of willing is obviously affected by its aptitudes. For this reason, when the human soul strongly wills something, it is said to be disposed to will that thing, or to will that thing affectionally.

The word "will" may be used equivocally to refer to three different things. There is, first, the instrument of willing, second, the affection of the instrument, and, third, the use of the instrument. The instrument of willing is that power of the soul which we use for willing—just as reason is the instrument of reasoning which we use when we reason, and sight is the instrument of seeing which we use when we see. The affection of the

11. Where "*aptitudines*" applies solely to the will (rather than to the hands, sight, etc.), the English words "inclinations" and "dispositions" better convey Anselm's idea.

instrument is that by which the instrument is disposed to will something even when a person is not thinking about it, so that when this thing comes to mind he either wills it immediately or for its own proper time. For example, the instrument of willing is so disposed to will good health (even when a person does not think about it) that as soon as this comes to mind he wills it immediately. And the will is so disposed to will sleep (even when a person does not think about it) that when it comes to mind he wills it for its own proper time. Never is the instrument of willing disposed to will sickness or to will never to sleep. In the same way, the instrument of the just man's will is, even while sleeping, so disposed to will justice that when he thinks of justice he immediately wills it. Finally, the use of the instrument of will is something we have only when we reflect upon the thing we are willing.

The word "will" is used to refer to all three of these: the instrument of willing, its affection, and its use. We call the instrument "will" in cases where we say that we direct the will toward various objects, such as toward willing to walk, and toward willing to sit, and toward willing now this, now that. Man always possesses this instrument even though he does not always use it—just as he has the power of sight, i.e., the instrument of seeing, even when (in his sleep, for instance) he is not using it. When he does use his sight he directs it sometimes toward seeing the sky, sometimes toward seeing the earth, and other times toward seeing other things. In the same way, we always possess reason, that is, the instrument of reasoning. We are not always using reason; but when we do use it we direct it toward different objects. Second, the affection of the instrument of willing is also called will. This usage occurs when we say that man always possesses the will for his own well-being. For here what we call will is the affection of that instrument by which a man wills well-being. In this way we say that a saint continually has the will to live justly, even when he is sleeping and not thinking about it. When we say that one person has more of the will to live justly than another person, the only will we are referring to is the affection of that instrument by which he wills to live justly. For the instrument is not greater in one person and less in another. Lastly, the use of this instrument is also called "will" when someone says, "I now have the will for reading," that is, "I now want to read"—or says, "I now have the will for writing," that is, "I now want to write." For just as seeing is using the sight which is the instrument of seeing, and just as its use is actual seeing, or sight (at least in the cases where "sight" signifies the same thing that "seeing" does, for "sight" can also signify the instrument of sight), so also willing is using the will which is the instrument of willing, and its use is the willing which occurs only when we think of what we are willing.

So, the will understood as the instrument is only one thing; that is, in a man the instrument of willing is only one thing, just as reason is only one thing, only a single instrument. But the will understood as that by which the instrument is affected has a double aspect. For just as sight has many aptitudes—such as the aptitude to see light, and through light to see figures, and in the figures to see color—so the instrument of willing has two aptitudes, which I call affections, or dispositions. One of these affections is for willing that which is beneficial (*commoditatem*), the other is for willing uprightness. For the will as instrument wills nothing except uprightness or what is beneficial. Whatever else it wills, it wills for the sake of one of these. And even when a man is mistaken in thinking that what he wills serves one of these ends, he nevertheless believes that it does. By the affection to will what is beneficial a man always wills happiness and being happy. By the affection to will uprightness he wills uprightness and being upright, or just. For the sake of what is beneficial he wills certain things, such as farming or laboring, in order to obtain the means to sustain life and health, which he regards as benefits. For the sake of uprightness he wills certain things, such as the toil of study, so that he may know how to live rightly, that is, justly. And finally, as we have already explained, the will understood as the use of our oft-mentioned instrument is actual only in those cases where the person reflects on what he wills. The divisions of this will are manifold; but we shall not deal with them now, though perhaps we shall return to them later.

Thus, "willing," like "seeing," has several meanings. The man who uses his sight and also the man who has the aptitude to see but does not use it are both said to see. In the same manner, the man who uses the instrument of willing while thinking about what he wills and the man who does not use it are both said to will, for the latter still has the affection, that is the aptitude, of willing.

That the word "will" indicates the instrument of willing, its affection, and its use, as three different wills, can also be recognized from the following consideration. If we can at the same time both affirm that a just man, even when he is sleeping and not reflecting on anything, has the will to live justly and deny that an unjust man has this will when he is sleeping, then we are denying of the unjust man the same will we are affirming in the just man. But obviously when we declare that the will to live justly is not in the unjust man who is sleeping, we are not denying that he has within him the will which I have called the instrument. For every man, asleep or awake, always has that will. Therefore, since this will, which we affirm to be in a good man, is the same as the will which we deny to be in an evil man, we mean by the will which is in a good man not the instrument but the will by which the instrument is affected. Furthermore, it is obvious that the will as use is never in a man when he is asleep (unless he is dreaming). For this reason, when we say that the will to live justly is in a just man while he is sleeping, we do not understand this to mean the use of the will. The will as affection, then, is neither the will as instrument nor the will as use. And everyone knows also that the will as instrument is different from the will as use; for when I say that I do not have the will to write, no one takes this to mean that I do not have the instrument for so willing. We may conclude, therefore, that "will" may mean variously an instrument, an affection, a use.[12]

The instrument of will moves all the other instruments which

12. In DL Anselm distinguishes only between will as instrument and will as use. DCD 13–14 discuss the will as affection without designating it as such. The present treatment is an explicit refinement of the view put forth in DCD.

we freely move—both those instruments that are a part of us (such as our hands, our tongue, our sight) and those that are independent of us (such as a pen or an ax). Furthermore, it causes all our voluntary movements; and it also moves itself by its affections. Hence, it may be called an instrument that moves itself. Now, I said that the instrument of will causes all voluntary actions. But when the matter is considered carefully, we find that it is more accurate to say that God causes everything which human nature or the human will does, for He creates the nature and the instrument of willing together with its affections, without which the instrument does nothing.

Chapter XII

A man's every merit, whether good or evil, derives from one or the other of the two affections, which we have called wills. These two wills differ from each other in that the will for what is beneficial is inseparable from the instrument of will; whereas the will for uprightness (as I said above) was originally separable from the instrument of will—separable, that is, for the angels and for our first parents, and still separable today for those men who are still in this life. These affections also differ in that the will which is the affection for willing what is beneficial is not itself the object that it wills, whereas the will which is the affection for willing uprightness *is* uprightness. For certainly no one wills uprightness unless he possesses uprightness; and no one can will uprightness except by means of uprightness. But it is clear that this uprightness belongs to the will considered as instrument. We mean this uprightness when we define "justice" as "uprightness of will kept for its own sake." And this uprightness is the truth of the will wherein the Lord charges Satan with not having remained steadfast, as I wrote in the dialogue *Concerning Truth*.

We must now consider how the merits of men—both those merits that lead to salvation and those that lead to condemnation—proceed from the two wills which I have called aptitudes, or affections. In itself uprightness is the cause of no evil but is the mother of every good merit. This uprightness aids the spirit in its striving against the flesh (Gal. 5:17) and delights "in the law of God after the inward man" (Rom. 7:22), that is, in accordance with the spirit which strives against the flesh. Even if evil sometimes seems to follow from uprightness, it does not really proceed from it but from something else. Because of their uprightness the apostles were a sweet savor to God (II Cor. 2:15). But the fact that the apostles were also a savor of death unto death for evil men, did not proceed from the justice of the apostles but from the wickedness of those evil men. Now, the affection for willing what is beneficial is not always evil, but it is evil when it gives assent to the flesh in its striving "against the spirit" (Gal. 5:17).

Chapter XIII

In order that we may understand this matter more clearly, we must investigate how this will for what is beneficial became so corrupt and prone to evil. For we must not believe that God created our first parents with such an affection toward evil. When I stated earlier that because of sin human nature became corrupt and acquired appetites similar to those of irrational animals, I did not explain how such a will arose in man; for base appetites are one thing, but a wicked will that assents to them is another. I think, therefore, that we must inquire how such a will became the lot of man.

The cause of such a will shall quickly become apparent to us if we consider the original condition of rational nature. The intention of God was to make rational nature just and happy, so that it could enjoy Him. But it was able to be neither just nor happy without the will for justice and happiness. Now, the will for justice is itself justice; but the will for happiness is not itself happiness, because not everyone who has the will for happiness has happiness. By common consent happiness is understood to include a sufficient degree of beneficial things without there being any want for more. And this is true whether one is thinking of the happiness of the angels or the happiness of Adam in

Paradise. Although the happiness of the angels exceeds that which belonged to Adam in Paradise, we cannot for this reason deny that Adam had happiness. For the fact that one object is very hot and is not at all cold does not exclude the existence of a second object even hotter. Or the fact that an object is very cold and is not at all hot does not mean that it cannot get even colder. By the same token, there was nothing to prevent Adam from being happy in Paradise and from having no want, even though the angels' happiness was greater than his. Having less of a thing than someone else has is not the same as being in need. For being in need consists in being deprived of something which one ought to have; but there was no deprivation in Adam. Where there is need there is wretchedness. God created rational nature to know and to love Him, and He did not make it wretched without some blame on its part. So, then, He created man happy and in need of nothing. Rational nature received at once (1) the will for happiness, and happiness, (2) the will for justice (i.e., it received uprightness, which is justice), (3) and free choice, without which it could not keep justice.

God has so ordained the two wills, or affections, that the instrument of will should use the affection for justice to order and govern one's choices under the guidance of the spirit, which is also called mind, or reason; and that it should use the other affection to will obedience without any disadvantage. Indeed, God gave happiness to man (not to mention the angels) for his benefit, but He gave man justice for His own honor. He gave justice, however, in such a way that man was able to desert it. But He also provided that if man did not desert it but persistently kept it, he would merit elevation to fellowship with the angels; but if he did desert it, he would subsequently have no way to recover it on his own. Moreover, if he did forsake it, he would fail to attain the happiness of the angels and, furthermore, would be deprived of the happiness which he did possess. As a further consequence, he would fall into the likeness of brute animals and become subject with them to corruption and to the appetites we have often mentioned. Nevertheless, the will for happiness would still remain, so that through a need of the good things which he had lost he would be justly punished with dire wretchedness. Therefore, since man actually did desert justice, he lost happiness. And the will (which was good when he received it and was designed for his own good) became fervent with desire for benefits it cannot now keep from willing because it cannot now have those true, but lost, benefits which are suitable for rational nature. In this condition the will turns itself to the false benefits sought by brute animals at the urging of their appetites. When the will wills these false benefits inordinately, then it either rejects uprightness, so that it does not receive it when offered, or else the will casts uprightness away once it has been received. But when the will wills these benefits within proper bounds, it does not shun or cast away uprightness.

In this manner, therefore, the instrument of will—created good in so far as it has being—was also created just and having the power to keep the uprightness it received. But it is made evil through free choice. It is then evil not in so far as it has being but in so far as it has been made unjust by the absence of the justice which it ought to have at all times but which it freely deserted. The will henceforth became powerless to will justice, which it had deserted. For through free choice one cannot will justice when he does not have it, although he can keep justice when he does have it. Moreover, the will for what is beneficial, which was created good in so far as it has being, becomes something evil; that is to say, it is made unjust because it is not subordinated to justice, without which it ought not to will anything. Therefore, the instrument of will freely became unjust; and in so far as it possessed any capability after it had deserted justice it was necessarily unjust and a servant of injustice. For it cannot return to justice by its own efforts. However, without justice the will can never actually be free, because without justice the natural freedom of choice is useless (*otiosa*). It is even made a servant to its own affection for what is beneficial; for once justice is taken away, a man can will only what this affection wills. I maintain that both the instrument and its affection actually will; for the instrument and the affection are both will, and so there is nothing incongruous in saying that both of them will. For it is true both that the instrument wills by its own affection and that the affection, through which the instrument wills, also wills (just as "seeing" refers both to the man who sees and also to the power of sight by which he sees). Hence, it is not absurd for us to say that the affections of the soul's instrument of will are, as it were, the instruments of that instrument—for the instrument of will operates only through its affections. So, then, after the will has lost its "instrument" for willing justice—that is, after the will has lost its uprightness—there is no way that it can will justice unless uprightness is restored to it by grace. And since the will ought not to will anything unless it can do so justly, whatever it wills without uprightness it wills unjustly. As for the appetites, all of which the Apostle calls the flesh, or concupiscence, they are not evil or unjust in so far as they have being; it is only in so far as they are found in rational creatures, where they do not belong, that they are called unjust. They are not evil or unjust in brute animals, because that is where they ought to be.

Chapter XIV

From all that I have said one can now see that man does not always possess the justice he ought always to have, because from himself he has no power or means to obtain or recover justice. It is also clear now that God causes good works solely through His own goodness, since He creates the will with free choice and gives it justice, by which to work good deeds. But the evil works God causes are attributable solely to man's blame, because God would not cause them if man did not will to do them. Nonetheless, God is the Author of their being, since He is the one who placed in man the will which man uses without justice. Therefore, it is man's fault alone, and not God's, that his deeds are evil, because God created in man a will with freedom of choice, and He bestowed justice on it, so that it would always will justly. So evil deeds are man's fault, because he deserted justice when he could have kept it. In regard to good works, God is responsible for the goodness which they have qua being, and also the goodness they have qua justice. But in regard to evil works, God is responsible only for the goodness which is theirs in so far as they have being; He is not responsible for the evil which is theirs through the absence of the justice they ought to have, which absence is not really something. When a man does good, he is responsible for the fact that his deeds are not evil. He is responsible because, when able to desert justice and do evil, he did not desert but kept uprightness through free choice, with the aid of grace—both the grace which is first given and that which comes subsequently. And when a man does evil, he is responsible only for the fact that his deeds are evil, because he does them of his own accord, that is, by his own unjust will.

I think that I can now fittingly bring to a close this treatise on these three difficult questions, a treatise which I began in the hope that God would help me. If what I have said here should prove to be a sufficient answer to any who might be inquiring about these matters, I cannot take the credit myself, because it was not I, but the grace of God with me, that accomplished this work. I will say this much, however. There was a time, when I was inquiring about these things, that my mind was wavering back and forth in its search for the right understanding of these problems. If someone had told me then the things that I have now written in this treatise, I would have thanked him, for he would have fully satisfied me. Accordingly, I was very much pleased with what God disclosed to me in this matter. And I thought that others would be similarly pleased if I wrote this treatise; for what I have freely received I wish to make freely available to those who are still seeking.

70 71 72 73   12 11 10 9 8 7 6 5 4 3 2 1